EXPERIENCE PORTUGAL

Unveiling Portugal's Timeless Treasures

DAVID JEREMIAH

Copyright © 2023 by David Jeremiah.

All rights reserved. No part of this publication may be reproduced, distributed, or transmitted in any form or by any means, including photocopying, recording, or other electronic or mechanical methods, without the prior written permission of the publisher, except in the case of brief quotations embodied in critical reviews and certain other noncommercial uses permitted by copyright law.

Table of Contents:

Introduction to Portugal — 5
Chapter 1: Welcome to Portugal — 7
- Geography and Climate — 10
- Cultural Overview — 14
- Etiquette — 18

Chapter 2: Planning Your Trip — 25
- Best Time to Visit — 28
- Visa and Travel Documents — 32
- Transportation in Portugal — 35
- Public Transportation — 40
- Renting a Car — 42
- Accommodation — 47
- Hotels and Resorts — 52
- Guesthouses and B&Bs — 58
- Hostels — 62
- Travel Itineraries — 67
- One Week Adventure — 71
- Two Weeks in the Heart of Portugal — 73
- Exploring the Algarve Coast — 76

Chapter 3: Exploring major cities — 79
Lisbon — 79
- Introduction to Lisbon — 80

Top Tourist Attractions — 81
- Belem Tower — 81
- Jeronimos Monastery — 83
- Alfama District — 86
- Vibrant Neighborhoods — 88

Culinary Delights	91
Nightlife and Entertainment	97
Porto and the North	**101**
Exploring Porto	101
Port Wine Cellars	103
Douro Valley	106
Braga and Guimarães	108
Central Portugal	**110**
Coimbra: The Ancient University City	113
Aveiro: The Venice of Portugal	115
Batalha, Alcobaça, and Tomar: Historical Monuments	**118**
Batalha	118
Alcobaça	120
Tomar	122
Serra da Estrela: The Highest Mountain Range	125
The Alentejo Region	**128**
Évora: A UNESCO Heritage City	130
Beja and Serpa: Off the Beaten Path	133
Cork and Wine Country	136
The Algarve: Sun, Sea, and Sand	**141**
Introduction to the Algarve	141
Beaches and Coastal Towns	142
Faro and Surroundings	146
Exploring the Rugged West Coast	150
Madeira and the Azores	**153**
Madeira Archipelago	155
Funchal: The Charming Capital	159

Nature and Outdoor Activities	161
The Azores Islands	164
São Miguel	166
Terceira	169
Pico and Faial	172
Chapter 4: Outdoor Adventures	**175**
Hiking and Trekking	175
Surfing and Watersports	178
Cycling Routes	182
Birdwatching and Wildlife Reserves	185
Chapter 5: Portuguese Cuisine and Wine	**189**
Traditional Dishes to Try	189
Iconic Portuguese Pastries	190
Wine Regions and Tasting Tours	193
Festivals and Cultural Events	197
Carnaval and Festas de Lisboa	201
Festa de São João in Porto	204
Folk Festivals in the Countryside	206
Chapter 6: Practical Tips for Travelers	**209**
Health and Safety	209
Money Matters	211
Language and Communication	215
Dos and Don'ts	218
Responsible Tourism Initiatives	222
Eco-friendly Accommodation	225
Chapter 7: Essential Portuguese Phrases	**229**
Basic Expressions	229
Shopping and Souvenirs	230

Introduction to Portugal

Portugal, located on the southwestern edge of Europe, is a captivating nation with a history that spans millennia. Bordered by Spain to the east and the vast Atlantic Ocean to the west, Portugal boasts a diverse landscape that ranges from rolling plains to rugged mountains and stunning coastlines. Its strategic position along major trade routes and maritime history have contributed to its cultural richness and global influence. With Lisbon as its capital, Portugal is a land of historical significance, dating back to the prehistoric era. The region was inhabited by various ancient civilizations, including the Phoenicians, Romans, and Moors, all of whom left their mark on the country's heritage. In the 15th and 16th centuries, Portugal's ambitious explorers set sail on daring expeditions that ushered in the

Age of Discovery, establishing trade routes to Africa, Asia, and the Americas.

Today, Portugal is a member of the European Union and has experienced significant economic and social development. Its stability and growing appeal as a tourist destination have placed it on the world stage, attracting travelers from all corners of the globe. Portugal is a captivating land of history, culture, and natural beauty. From its maritime legacy to its delectable cuisine and warm hospitality, Portugal offers an enriching experience for those seeking to discover a country that embraces both its past and future with pride. Whether exploring the charming streets of Lisbon or basking in the coastal splendor of the Algarve, Portugal invites visitors to immerse themselves in its unique charm and create cherished memories that will last a lifetime.

Chapter 1: Welcome to Portugal

Welcome to Portugal, a land of captivating beauty, rich history, and warm hospitality! Nestled in the southwestern corner of Europe, Portugal is a country that holds a special place in the hearts of travelers from around the world. From its golden coastlines to its charming countryside, Portugal offers a diverse array of experiences that will leave visitors enchanted. As you step foot onto Portuguese soil, you'll be greeted by a delightful blend of traditional and modern influences. The country's cities are vibrant and bustling, with

Lisbon, the capital, standing tall as a captivating metropolis. Wander through its historic neighborhoods, such as Alfama, where narrow cobblestone streets wind through ancient buildings adorned with colorful tiles, revealing glimpses of a bygone era. Don't miss the iconic Belém Tower and Jerónimos Monastery, both UNESCO World Heritage sites, showcasing Portugal's illustrious past. Venturing north, Porto beckons you with its undeniable charm. Famous for its production of port wine, this city is nestled along the Douro River and boasts an enchanting old town, Ribeira, which offers postcard-worthy views of the riverfront. Sip on a glass of port wine, indulge in delectable local cuisine, and soak in the lively atmosphere of this captivating city. While the cities offer a vibrant experience, Portugal's natural wonders are equally alluring. The Algarve, Portugal's southernmost region, boasts stunning golden beaches, dramatic cliffs, and crystal-clear waters. From the bustling resorts to secluded coves, the Algarve caters to every type of beachgoer. If you seek tranquility and a taste of rural life, head inland to explore the charming villages and rolling vineyards of the Douro Valley. Known for producing the famous port wine, this region will charm you with its serene landscapes and warm, welcoming locals. For history enthusiasts, a journey to Sintra is a must. This magical town is dotted with fairytale-like castles and palaces, including the colorful Pena Palace, set atop a hill overlooking lush forests.

Sintra's romantic ambiance has inspired poets and writers for centuries, and it continues to captivate visitors today.

Beyond the mainland, Portugal's archipelagos, the Azores and Madeira, beckon adventurers with their volcanic landscapes, diverse flora and fauna, and opportunities for hiking, diving, and other outdoor activities. These island paradises offer a unique experience away from the mainland's hustle and bustle. No trip to Portugal would be complete without savoring its delicious cuisine. Seafood lovers will be in heaven as they indulge in fresh catches from the Atlantic Ocean, while foodies will relish traditional dishes like (salted cod) and pastéis de nata (custard tarts). Pair your meals with a selection of local wines and you're in for a true culinary delight. Portugal's people are renowned for their warmth and friendliness, and you'll find the locals eager to share their culture and traditions with you. Whether you're engaging in lively conversations over coffee or witnessing a spirited fado performance, the Portuguese passion for life is contagious.

So, welcome to Portugal, a country that effortlessly weaves together its historical legacy, natural splendor, and cultural treasures. Prepare to be enchanted by its beauty, moved by its history, and embraced by its people as you embark on an unforgettable journey through this captivating nation. Boa ! (Have a good trip!)

Geography and Climate

Portugal, located in the southwestern part of Europe on the Iberian Peninsula, shares its borders with Spain to the east and north and is surrounded by the Atlantic Ocean to the west and south. The country has a diverse geography that includes a long coastline, mountains, river valleys, and two island groups.

Coastline:
Portugal boasts a coastline that stretches approximately 1,794 kilometers (1,115 miles) along the Atlantic Ocean. The coastline is characterized by a mix of sandy beaches, rocky cliffs, and charming coves. The southern region, known as the Algarve, is renowned for its beautiful golden beaches and a Mediterranean climate that attracts

tourists from around the world. In the western part of Portugal, the Silver Coast offers a more rugged and wild landscape, attracting surfers and nature enthusiasts.

Mountains:
The northern and central regions of Portugal are dominated by mountainous terrain. The highest mountain range in mainland Portugal is the Serra da Estrela, with its highest peak, Torre, rising to 1,993 meters (6,539 feet) above sea level. The landscape here is characterized by deep valleys, dense forests, and granite peaks. The northern region is also home to the Peneda-Gerês National Park, Portugal's only national park, offering stunning natural beauty and abundant wildlife.

River Valleys:

Several major rivers flow through Portugal, contributing to its fertile valleys and supporting agriculture. The most significant river is the Tagus (Rio Tejo), which runs through the capital city, Lisbon, before reaching the Atlantic Ocean. The Douro River, in the north, is famous for its picturesque terraced valleys and its role in producing renowned port wine.

Islands:

Portugal is home to two archipelagos in the Atlantic Ocean: the Azores and Madeira. The Azores consist of nine volcanic islands located around 1,500 kilometers (930 miles) west of the mainland. They offer stunning landscapes, including volcanic craters, lakes, and lush greenery. Madeira, situated approximately 1,000 kilometers (620 miles) southwest of Portugal, is also of volcanic origin and has a subtropical climate, characterized by steep cliffs, terraced farmlands, and beautiful gardens.

Climate of Portugal:

Portugal experiences a Mediterranean climate in the southern regions and a more temperate maritime climate in the northern parts. The Azores and Madeira have their own distinct microclimates due to their isolated locations in the Atlantic Ocean.

Mediterranean Climate (Southern Portugal):
The southern regions, including the Algarve, have a Mediterranean climate. Summers are hot and dry, with average temperatures ranging from 25°C to 30°C (77°F to 86°F) and sometimes even higher. Winters are mild, with temperatures averaging around 10°C to 15°C (50°F to 59°F). Rainfall is scarce during the summer months, but winters can bring some precipitation.

Temperate Maritime Climate (Northern Portugal):
Central and northern Portugal experience a temperate maritime climate. Summers are generally warm with average temperatures between 20°C and 25°C (68°F to 77°F). Winters are cooler, with temperatures ranging from 8°C to 15°C (46°F to 59°F). The northern regions receive more rainfall throughout the year compared to the south.

Azores and Madeira:
The Azores and Madeira have mild, subtropical climates due to their oceanic influences. These regions experience relatively stable temperatures throughout the year, with average highs ranging from 17°C to 26°C (63°F to 79°F) in Madeira and 15°C to 25°C (59°F to 77°F) in the Azores. Rainfall can be significant, especially during the winter months.

Portugal's geography and climate offer a diverse and captivating environment. From its beautiful coastline to its mountainous landscapes and unique islands, Portugal has something to offer for every nature lover and traveler seeking a variety of experiences. Whether exploring the sandy beaches of the Algarve, hiking in the lush forests of the Serra da Estrela, or enjoying the mild climate of Madeira, Portugal has a rich tapestry of natural beauty to be explored.

Cultural Overview

Portugal's cultural overview is a fascinating blend of its rich history, diverse influences, and vibrant traditions. Located on the Iberian Peninsula, Portugal's culture has been shaped by its geographical position and its interactions with various civilizations throughout the centuries. Here's a closer look at the cultural aspects that define Portugal:

History and Heritage: Portugal has a deep and significant history that dates back to ancient times. It was a Roman province, and later, during the 8th century, the Moors from North Africa ruled parts of the Iberian Peninsula, including present-day Portugal. In the 12th century, Portugal gained its independence, and the country's golden age was during the Age of Exploration in the 15th and 16th centuries. The legacy of this past is evident in the historical landmarks, palaces, and castles scattered across the country.

Language and Literature: The Portuguese language is the backbone of Portugal's cultural identity. As one of the most widely spoken languages in the world, Portuguese has deep historical roots and has spread to various regions through colonial expeditions. Portuguese literature has produced influential authors and poets, with classics like "Os Lusíadas" by Luís de Camões and the works of Fernando Pessoa gaining international recognition.

Fado Music: Fado is an iconic music genre that expresses the soul and emotions of the Portuguese people. It originated in the early 19th century in the city of Lisbon and has since become an essential part of Portugal's cultural heritage. Fado songs often revolve around themes of longing, nostalgia, and the struggles of life, creating a haunting and melancholic atmosphere that resonates with listeners.

Cuisine:Portuguese cuisine is a delightful fusion of flavors, influenced by the country's maritime history and diverse regional produce. Seafood, particularly cod, is a staple, and Portugal's love affair with "bacalhau" has earned it the nickname "the country of a thousand cod recipes." Other dishes like " verde" (kale soup), "francesinha" (a hearty sandwich), and an array of delectable pastries contribute to Portugal's reputation as a food lover's paradise.

Architecture: Portugal boasts an impressive array of architectural styles. Romanesque, Gothic, Manueline, Renaissance, and Baroque elements are visible in historic buildings and monuments. The intricate "azulejos," or decorative tiles, are a prominent feature on walls and facades, adding a unique touch to Portuguese architecture. Notable examples include the Tower of Belém, Jerónimos Monastery, and the Pena Palace.

Religious Celebrations: Religion, particularly Roman Catholicism, has profoundly influenced Portuguese culture and traditions. Religious festivals and processions, such as Easter celebrations and the Feast of St. Anthony, are vibrant and deeply rooted in the lives of the people. Many towns and villages hold religious events, attracting both locals and visitors alike.

Festivals and Celebrations: Portugal is known for its lively festivals and celebrations. The annual Carnival festivities bring colorful parades and street parties across the country, while local festivals celebrate regional traditions, saints, and historical events. One of the most famous festivals is the

"Feast of São João" in Porto, where locals take to the streets with sardines, dancing, and fireworks.

Arts and Crafts: Portugal has a rich tradition of arts and crafts, with pottery, embroidery, and hand-painted tiles being notable examples. Traditional handicrafts showcase a deep connection to local culture and heritage, and many artisans continue to preserve these traditions.

Sports: Football (soccer) is a national passion, and the Portuguese are avid sports enthusiasts.

Portugal has produced world-class footballers like Cristiano Ronaldo, elevating the country's status in the international sports arena.

Overall, Portugal's cultural overview is a captivating journey through time, where ancient traditions and modern influences coexist harmoniously. The warmth and hospitality of the Portuguese people, coupled with the nation's breathtaking landscapes and historical treasures, make it a captivating destination for travelers seeking an enriching cultural experience.

Etiquette

Etiquette in Portugal is deeply rooted in the country's rich history, traditions, and strong sense of community. Portuguese people value politeness, warmth, and respect in their interactions, whether with friends, family, colleagues, or strangers. Understanding and adhering to the following comprehensive etiquette guidelines can help you navigate social situations in Portugal with ease and appreciation for the local customs:

Greetings and Introductions:
- When meeting someone for the first time or entering a room, it's customary to greet with a handshake or a kiss on both cheeks (air kiss) if you're familiar with the person. Handshakes are more common in formal situations.
- Use formal titles like "Senhor" (Mr.) and "Senhora" (Mrs./Ms.) when addressing people, especially in business or formal settings.
- Address older individuals or those in positions of authority with appropriate titles and last names.

Personal Space and Gestures:
- Portuguese people value personal space, so avoid standing too close to others during conversations.
- Avoid excessive gesturing or touching, especially with people you don't know well.

Punctuality:
- Being on time is generally appreciated, especially for business meetings and formal events.
- In more casual and social settings, such as gatherings with friends, there may be a more relaxed approach to time, and people might arrive a bit late.

Dining Etiquette:
- Wait for the host to start the meal before you begin eating.
- Keep your hands visible on the table while dining, and finish everything on your plate as wasting food may be seen as impolite.
- Refusing food or drink may also be considered impolite, so it's best to accept at least a small portion.

Gift-Giving:
- When invited to someone's home, it's a kind gesture to bring a small gift for the host.

Flowers, chocolates, or a bottle of wine are popular choices.
- Avoid lilies and chrysanthemums as they are associated with funerals.
- If you receive a gift, express gratitude with a genuine smile and a thank-you note or call.

Dress Code:
- Portuguese people generally dress smartly, especially in urban areas.
- Dress modestly and conservatively when visiting religious sites or attending formal events.
- Beachwear is appropriate only for the beach or pool areas, not in public places.

Language:
- While many Portuguese people speak English, making an effort to learn a few basic Portuguese phrases will be appreciated and show respect for the local culture.
- Addressing people in Portuguese, even with simple greetings like "Bom dia" (Good morning) or "Obrigado/a" (Thank you), can create a positive impression.

Conversations and Topics:
- Portuguese people are generally friendly and enjoy engaging in conversations.
- Common topics include family, soccer (football), food, and cultural events.
- Be cautious when discussing sensitive subjects like politics or religion, especially with people you don't know well, to avoid potential disagreements.

Tipping:
- Tipping is not obligatory in Portugal, as a service charge is often included in the bill. However, leaving a small tip for exceptional service (usually 5-10% of the bill) is appreciated.

Socializing and Hospitality:
- Portuguese people are known for their warm hospitality and may invite you to their

homes for meals or social gatherings. Accepting such invitations is a great way to experience local culture.
- At social events, engage in conversations, and show interest in the traditions and customs of Portugal.

Saying Goodbye:
- When leaving a social gathering or event, it's customary to say goodbye to each person individually, either with a handshake or a kiss on both cheeks.

Remember that while these etiquette guidelines provide a general overview of Portuguese customs, there might be some regional variations and individual preferences. The key to successful interactions in Portugal is showing respect, warmth, and an open-minded approach to embracing the local culture and customs.

Chapter 2: Planning Your Trip

Planning a trip to Portugal promises an indelible adventure filled with rich history, startling geographies, succulent cookery, and warm hospitality. As you start disposing your trip to this witching country, then are some essential tips to make the utmost of your experience:

Decide on Your Itinerary: Portugal offers a different range of lodestones, from the major thoroughfares of Lisbon to the graphic strands of the Algarve, the stations of the Douro Valley, and the medieval fetish of Porto. Determine the metropolises and regions you want to visit, esteeming the duration of your trip and your interests.

Perfect Time to Visit: Portugal has a Mediterranean climate with mild layoffs and hot summers. The peak sightseer season is during the summer months(June to August), when the rainfall is warm and bright. Still, spring(April to June) and fall(September to October) are also excellent moments to visit, with affable temperatures and smaller crowds.

Transportation: Portugal has an effective and well-connected transportation system. Major metropolises are linked by trains and motorcars, and the country's airfields serve transnational and domestic breakouts. Leasing an auto is also a popular option, especially if you want to explore remote areas or the country.

Accommodation: Portugal offers a wide range of accommodation options, from sumptuous hospices and resorts to canny guesthouses and account- friendly caravansaries . Bespeak your accommodation in advance, especially during the peak season, to secure the stylish options and classes.

Language: Portuguese is the general language of Portugal. While English is extensively stated in sightseer areas, mastering many introductory Portuguese expressions can enhance your experience and show off reference for the original cultivation.

Currency and Payment: The currency exercised in Portugal is the Euro(EUR). Credence cards are extensively accepted, but it's a good idea to bear some cash, especially for lower joints and original requests.

Safety and Health: Portugal is usually a safe country for trippers. Still, as with any destination, it's essential to stay watchful, especially in loaded sightseer areas, to shake pickpocketing. ensure you have trip insurance that covers any medical extremities during your trip.

Must- Visit Destinations: Some of the must-have-stay destinations in Portugal carry
- **Lisbon**: Portugal's vibrant capital, offering a mix of history, cultivation, and fustiness.
- **Porto**: Known for its harborage wine, literal armature, and scenic Douro River views.
- **Sintra**: A fairytale city with startling palaces and prosperous auditoriums , fluently popular from Lisbon.
- **Algarve**: Famous for its startling bank, rosy strands, and graphic fishing townlets.

27

- Coimbra: Home to one of the world's oldest universities and a rich artistic rubric.
- **Douro Valley:** A UNESCO World Heritage Site famed for its terraced stations and wine products.

Local Cuisine: Portugal is a food nut's Eden. Do not miss trying traditional dishes like Pastéis de Nata(custard cocottes), Bacalhau(interspersed cod), Francesinha(a hearty sandwich), and the colorful seafood delectables. Brace your reflections with original wines and harborage for an authentic culinary experience.

Cultural Etiquette: Portuguese people are friendly and sociable. When visiting literal spots or churches, dress abjectly. Also, tilting isn't mandatory but accelerated for good indulgence. With these tips in mind, your trip to Portugal is bound to be an enriching and pleasurable experience, creating cherished recollections that will survive a continuance.

Best Time to Visit

The best time to visit a destination often depends on various factors, including weather, activities, crowds, and personal preferences. For Portugal, different seasons offer unique experiences, so choosing the right time to visit depends on what you want to get out of your trip. Here's a breakdown of the seasons to help you decide the best time to visit Portugal:

1. Spring (April to June):
Spring is a fantastic time to visit Portugal, particularly from mid-April to early June. During this season, the weather starts to warm up, and the landscapes come alive with colorful flowers and blossoms. The temperatures are generally pleasant, ranging from mild to warm, making it ideal for exploring cities, historical sites, and coastal areas without the scorching summer heat. One significant advantage of visiting during spring is the fewer crowds compared to the peak summer season. You'll have a more relaxed and authentic experience, especially in popular tourist destinations.

2. Summer (July to August):
Summer is the high tourist season in Portugal, particularly in July and August. The weather is hot and dry, making it perfect for enjoying the beautiful beaches along the coast. However, temperatures can soar, especially in inland regions.

While the summer offers long sunny days and a vibrant atmosphere, it also means larger crowds and higher prices for accommodations and tourist activities. If you prefer a lively ambiance, beach parties, and an abundance of festivals, summer might be the best time for you.

3. Fall (September to October):
Fall is another excellent time to visit Portugal, especially from mid-September to mid-October. The weather remains pleasant, and the summer crowds

start to dwindle, providing a more peaceful and authentic experience. This season is perfect for exploring cities, indulging in outdoor activities, and visiting vineyards during the grape harvest season.
The fall foliage is also stunning in some areas, particularly in the northern regions, adding an extra touch of beauty to your travel experience.

4. Winter (November to March):
Winter in Portugal is mild along the coast, but temperatures can drop significantly in the northern and inland regions. While it might not be the best time for beach activities, winter can still be an appealing season for cultural exploration and sightseeing. Cities like Lisbon and Porto are less crowded during winter, and you can explore the historical sites and museums at a more leisurely pace. Additionally, winter is an excellent time for food enthusiasts to enjoy hearty traditional dishes and warm drinks.

The best time to visit Portugal depends on your preferences. If you prefer milder weather and fewer crowds, consider visiting during spring or fall. If you love the lively atmosphere, hot weather, and beach activities, then the summer months are ideal. And for those who enjoy cultural experiences and sightseeing without the summer hustle, winter can be a charming time to explore Portugal's history and culinary delights.

Visa and Travel Documents

Still, please note that visa and trip regulations might change over time, so it's essential to corroborate the most up- to- date information with the sanctioned Portuguese government or applicable authorities before making any trip plans.

- **Visa Conditions**: Portugal is a member of the European Union(EU) and the Schengen Area, which means that the visa conditions for Portugal are aligned with the Schengen visa policy.
- **Schengen Visa:** If you're a citizen of a country that isn't pure from the Schengen visa demand, you'll need to apply for a Schengen visa to visit Portugal for tourism, business, or family visits for over 90 days within a 180- day period. The Schengen visa allows you to travel to all the 26 Schengen Area countries, including Portugal.
- **Short- stay Visa:** The Schengen visa is a short- stay visa, meaning it's intended for temporary stays. It doesn't grant you the right to work or live in Portugal beyond the 90- day limit.
- **Long- stay Visa(National Visa):** If you plan to stay in Portugal for further than 90 days or wish to work, study, or join family members abiding in Portugal, you'll need to apply for a long- stay visa, also known as a public visa. The public visa is specific to Portugal and doesn't grant access to other Schengen countries for long- term stays.

- **Visa- Exempt Countries:** Citizens of certain countries are exempt from the Schengen visa demand for short stays in Portugal and other Schengen countries. They can enter Portugal visa-free for over 90 days within a 180- day period. The list of visa-free countries can change over time.

Trip Documents:

Passport: Anyhow of your nation, you'll need a valid passport to travel to Portugal. ensure that your passport is valid for at least three months beyond your intended departure date from the Schengen area.

- **Travel Insurance**: While it isn't a formal trip document, having trip insurance is largely recommended when visiting Portugal. trip insurance can give content for medical extremities, trip cancellations, lost baggage, and other unlooked-for events during your trip.
- **Evidence of Accommodation and Sufficient finances:** Immigration authorities may ask for substantiation of accommodation arrangements for your stay in Portugal and sufficient fiscal means to cover your charges during your visit.

- **Operation Process**: To apply for a visa to Portugal, you'll need to visit the Portuguese consulate or delegation in your country of hearthstone. The operation process and needed documents may vary depending on the type of visa you're applying for and your nation. It's judicious to start the operation process well in advance of your planned trip dates. Always corroborate the current visa and trip conditions with the sanctioned Portuguese government websites or consular services before making any trip arrangements.

Transportation in Portugal

Transportation in Portugal is well-developed and efficient, offering a variety of options to both residents and tourists. The country's transportation system encompasses various modes of travel, including road networks, railways, air travel, and public transportation, all of which are interconnected to facilitate easy movement throughout the country and beyond.

Road Transport: Portugal has an extensive network of well-maintained roads and highways, making road travel a popular choice for both locals and visitors. The major highways are known as "," and they connect major cities and regions, allowing for swift and comfortable journeys. Toll roads are also prevalent, and while they can add to the cost of travel, they often provide faster routes and better road conditions. Secondary roads provide access to smaller towns and picturesque rural areas.

Rail Transport: The Portuguese rail network, operated by "Comboios de Portugal" (CP), is efficient and covers most of the country. Trains are a reliable and comfortable way to travel between major cities and regions. The main railway line connects Lisbon in the south to Porto in the north, with several stops along the way, including Coimbra and Aveiro. High-speed trains, known as "Alfa Pendular," offer quicker connections between Lisbon and Porto, reducing travel time significantly.

Public Transportation: Major cities in Portugal, such as Lisbon, Porto, and Coimbra, have well-developed public transportation systems. These typically include buses, trams, and metro services that provide convenient and affordable travel within urban areas. In cities like Lisbon, the iconic yellow trams add a touch of charm to the cityscape while facilitating easy transportation for locals and tourists alike.

Air Travel: Portugal is served by several international airports, with Lisbon Portela Airport being the largest and busiest. Other significant airports include Porto Francisco Sá Carneiro Airport, Faro Airport, and Madeira Airport. These airports connect Portugal to numerous destinations worldwide, making air travel a convenient choice for those traveling from farther distances.

Sea Transport: Given its extensive coastline, Portugal has a significant maritime tradition, and several ports serve as hubs for both passenger and cargo ships. The port of Lisbon, for instance, is an essential stop for many cruise liners, offering tourists a gateway to explore the country and its neighboring regions.

Public Transport Cards: To enhance the convenience of public transportation, many cities in Portugal offer reloadable travel cards that can be used across different modes of transport. These cards provide discounted fares and are particularly helpful for regular commuters and tourists exploring the cities.

Ridesharing and Taxis: Ridesharing services like Uber and Bolt are available in major Portuguese cities, providing an additional option for point-to-point travel. Traditional taxis are also widely available and easily recognizable by their distinctive black color.
Overall, Portugal's transportation infrastructure is modern and reliable, making it relatively easy to

traverse the country. Whether it's exploring the scenic coastline, historic cities, or charming rural areas, travelers have access to various transportation options that cater to different preferences and budgets.

Public Transportation

Public transportation in Portugal is an integral part of the country's transportation network, providing efficient and accessible options for both locals and tourists. The country's public transit system is well-developed, connecting major cities, towns, and rural areas, making it convenient for people to travel throughout the country.

Trains: The Portuguese railway system, operated by Comboios de Portugal (CP), is one of the most popular modes of long-distance transportation. The trains are reliable, comfortable, and offer an excellent way to travel between major cities like Lisbon, Porto, Coimbra, Faro, and others. High-speed Alfa Pendular trains connect Lisbon to Porto, reducing travel times significantly. The scenic Douro and Alentejo lines are popular among tourists for their breathtaking views of the countryside.

Metro: Major cities like Lisbon and Porto have modern metro systems that provide a quick and efficient way to navigate within the urban areas. The Lisbon Metro, for example, has four lines covering various parts of the city and surrounding suburbs. Porto's metro system also serves the city and extends to neighboring areas, enhancing connectivity and reducing road traffic.

Buses: The bus network in Portugal is extensive, linking cities, towns, and villages across the country. Rede Expressos and Rodoviária are two major bus companies that offer long-distance and intercity services. Regional and local buses provide connectivity within smaller towns and rural regions, ensuring that even remote areas remain accessible.

Trams: Lisbon, known for its charming hills and historic neighborhoods, has iconic trams running through its streets. Tram 28, in particular, is a famous route that takes tourists on a picturesque journey through the city's most scenic spots. Trams are not just a mode of transportation but also an attraction in themselves, adding to the overall experience of exploring Lisbon.

Ferries: Portugal's coastal location means that ferries are an important part of its public transportation system, especially in regions like Lisbon and Porto. Ferries connect Lisbon to the southern bank of the Tagus River, and in Porto, they transport people across the Douro River. Additionally, there are ferry services between mainland Portugal and the Azores and Madeira islands.

Shared Mobility: In recent years, Portugal has seen an increase in shared mobility options like bike-sharing and electric scooters in urban areas.

These initiatives promote eco-friendly transportation and offer flexible options for short trips, complementing the existing public transit system.

Integrated Ticketing: Many regions in Portugal have adopted integrated ticketing systems, allowing passengers to use a single ticket for multiple modes of public transportation. This convenience makes it easier for travelers to switch between trains, buses, metros, and trams without the hassle of purchasing separate tickets for each leg of their journey. Overall, public transportation in Portugal is well-regarded for its reliability, affordability, and coverage of both urban centers and rural areas. The government's efforts to invest in modernizing and expanding the transportation infrastructure have made traveling around the country convenient and accessible to all, making public transit an excellent choice for exploring the beauty and culture of Portugal.

Renting a Car

Renting a car in Portugal can be a fantastic way to explore this beautiful country at your own pace, giving you the freedom to visit remote villages, scenic coastal drives, and historic landmarks that may not be easily accessible by public transportation. Here's a guide to help you navigate the process of renting a car in Portugal:

- Driving License Requirements:To rent a car in Portugal, you must have a valid driver's license from your home country. Most car rental companies accept international driving licenses, but it's always a good idea to check with the specific company beforehand.

- Age Restrictions: Generally, the minimum age for renting a car in Portugal is 21 years old. However, some rental companies may require drivers to be at least 23 or even 25 years old. Young driver surcharges may apply if you're under 25, so be sure to inquire about this when booking your car.

- Booking in Advance: It's recommended to book your rental car in advance, especially during peak tourist seasons or holidays when demand can be high. Online platforms and rental car websites are convenient ways to compare prices and find the best deals.

Choosing the Right Car: Consider the number of passengers and the amount of luggage you'll have when selecting a car. If you plan to explore rural areas or hilly regions, renting a car with more power and space might be beneficial. Conversely, if you're exploring cities, a smaller car could be easier to park.

Insurance: Basic insurance is usually included in the rental price, but it's essential to understand the coverage and any deductible amount. Car rental companies may offer additional insurance options to reduce or eliminate the deductible. Review the terms and conditions carefully to ensure you have the coverage you're comfortable with.Fuel Policy: Most rental companies provide the car with a full tank of fuel, and you'll be required to return it with a full tank as well. Make sure to locate nearby gas stations before returning the vehicle to avoid unnecessary feel. Toll Roads: Portugal has a good network of toll roads. Some rental cars come with an electronic toll device, while others may require you to pay cash at toll booths. Clarify with the rental company about their toll policy to avoid fines or administrative fees.

Parking: Parking in cities and tourist areas can be limited and expensive. Be prepared to pay for parking or look for free parking areas outside the city centers. Blue zones often require payment for parking, while white zones are usually free.

Driving Rules: Familiarize yourself with the local driving rules and regulations in Portugal. For example, seat belts are mandatory for all passengers, and the use of mobile phones while driving is prohibited unless using hands-free devices.

GPS or Navigation: Consider renting a GPS device or use a reliable navigation app on your smartphone to help you navigate Portugal's roads easily.

Inspect the Car: Before leaving the rental car facility, thoroughly inspect the vehicle for any existing damages, and point them out to the rental company to avoid being held responsible for pre-existing issues upon return.

There are numerous car rental companies in Portugal, including both international chains and local providers. Here is a list of some well-known car rental companies that operate in Portugal:

Europcar: Europcar is a well-established car rental company with locations throughout Portugal, including major airports and cities.

Hertz: Hertz is another popular international car rental company offering services in Portugal. They have offices at major airports and city centers.

Avis: Avis is a well-known car rental brand with a presence in Portugal, providing a wide range of vehicles for rent.

Sixt: Sixt is a global car rental company that operates in Portugal, offering various car categories to suit different needs.

Budget: Budget is a budget-friendly car rental option with multiple locations in Portugal, making it convenient for travelers.

Enterprise: Enterprise Rent-A-Car has branches across Portugal, providing rental solutions for both leisure and business travelers.

Alamo: Alamo Rent A Car is part of the same company as Enterprise and offers car rental services at various locations in Portugal.

Guerin: Guerin is a Portuguese car rental company with a broad network of locations across the country.

Goldcar: Goldcar is a popular option for budget-conscious travelers, and they have offices at major airports and tourist destinations.

Drive on Holidays: A local car rental company that offers personalized services with a range of car options.

Auto Jardim: With over 40 locations in Portugal, Auto Jardim provides car rental services in multiple cities and tourist areas.

Bravacar: Bravacar is a local car rental company with branches in Lisbon, Faro, and Porto, among other locations.

Always remember to compare prices, read customer reviews, and check the terms and conditions before finalizing your rental car booking. Additionally, booking in advance often leads to better deals and availability, especially during peak travel seasons. Renting a car in Portugal can be a rewarding experience, offering you the chance to explore the country's stunning landscapes, historical sites, and vibrant cities on your own terms. Just remember to plan ahead, drive safely, and enjoy the journey!

Accommodation

Accommodation in Portugal offers a wide array of options to suit various preferences and budgets, making it an attractive destination for tourists from around the world. As a country with diverse landscapes, rich history, and a vibrant culture, Portugal offers an array of accommodation choices, ranging from luxury hotels to budget-friendly hostels, charming guesthouses, and traditional vacation rentals.

Hotels: Portugal boasts numerous luxury hotels in major cities like Lisbon, Porto, and Faro, as well as in picturesque regions like the Algarve and Douro Valley. These hotels often feature world-class amenities such as spa facilities, gourmet restaurants, swimming pools, and stunning views. Many hotels also reflect Portugal's history and architecture, blending modern comforts with traditional charm.

Guesthouses/Pousadas: For travelers seeking a more intimate and authentic experience, Portugal's guesthouses or "pousadas" are an excellent choice. Pousadas are typically small, family-run establishments, often set in historic buildings like castles, monasteries, or traditional houses. Staying in a pousada allows visitors to immerse themselves in the country's cultural heritage and enjoy personalized attention.

Vacation Rentals: Renting apartments, villas, or cottages has become increasingly popular in Portugal, especially for families or larger groups. This option offers more space and privacy, and it allows travelers to experience the local lifestyle by shopping at nearby markets and preparing their meals. Many vacation rentals are available in popular tourist regions like the Algarve and Madeira.

Hostels: Portugal is known for its friendly and sociable atmosphere, making hostels an ideal choice for budget-conscious travelers or those seeking to meet fellow backpackers. Major cities and tourist destinations have a plethora of well-maintained hostels with shared dormitories and private rooms. Hostels often organize social events, making it easy for travelers to connect and explore together.

Pensions and Residenciais: These are small, family-run accommodations similar to guesthouses but with a simpler setup. Pensions and residenciais are scattered throughout the country, offering affordable and basic lodging, perfect for travelers looking for a more traditional Portuguese experience.

Rural Tourism (Turismo Rural): For those who want to escape the hustle and bustle of cities, Portugal's rural tourism accommodations are a fantastic choice. These properties are typically situated in the countryside or in small villages, providing a tranquil and authentic experience of the Portuguese way of life.

Camping: Portugal's beautiful natural landscapes make camping an attractive option for nature enthusiasts. There are numerous campsites equipped with facilities for tents, campervans, and caravans across the country. Some campsites are located near beaches, while others are nestled in lush forests or near picturesque lakes.

Regardless of the type of accommodation chosen, travelers to Portugal can expect warm hospitality, delicious cuisine, and a wealth of cultural experiences. Whether you're exploring historic sites in Lisbon, savoring the world-famous port wine in Porto, or relaxing on the stunning beaches of the Algarve, Portugal's accommodation options cater to a diverse range of preferences, making it a memorable destination for all kinds of travelers.

Hotels and Resorts

Please note that the availability and pricing of hotels and resorts can vary depending on the season and demand. here is a list of some affordable hotels and resorts in Portugal:

Lisbon
- Hotel Luena: A budget-friendly hotel in the heart of Lisbon, offering comfortable rooms

and a convenient location close to public transportation and major attractions.
- Hotel Mundial: Situated in the Baixa district, this hotel provides affordable accommodations with rooftop views of the city.

Porto:
- **Moov Hotel Porto Centro:** Located in Porto's city center, this modern and budget-conscious hotel offers a great base for exploring the city's historic sites and cultural landmarks.
- **Star Inn Porto:** A contemporary and affordable option with comfortable rooms, situated near the Porto Airport and the Norte Shopping Center.

Faro:
- **Stay Hotel Faro Centro**: A budget hotel in Faro's city center, offering a convenient location for exploring the Algarve region.
- **Hotel Eva:** While not the cheapest option, it can offer affordable rates during certain periods, and it boasts a great location overlooking the marina.

Algarve:
- Luna Alpinus Hotel: Located in Albufeira, this hotel offers comfortable

accommodations and access to nearby beaches at a reasonable price.
- Quinta Pedra dos Bicos: Situated in the popular resort town of Albufeira, this budget-friendly hotel provides easy access to the beautiful Praia da Oura beach.

Madeira:
- The Lince Madeira Lido Atlantic Great Hotel: This hotel in Funchal offers affordable rates and is close to the city's main attractions and the scenic Lido Promenade.
- Hotel Orquídea: Located in the heart of Funchal, this hotel provides budget-friendly rooms and is within walking distance of many restaurants and shops.

Azores:
- Hotel Ponta Delgada: This hotel in Ponta Delgada on São Miguel Island offers affordable rates and a central location to explore the island's natural beauty.
- Hotel Talisman**: While not the most budget-conscious, it can offer competitive rates during certain times and provides a charming stay in Ponta Delgada.

Here's a list of other well-known hotels and resorts in Portugal, each offering unique experiences and amenities for travelers:

- Pestana Palace Lisboa (Lisbon): A luxurious 5-star hotel housed in a 19th-century palace, offering elegant rooms, beautiful gardens, a spa, and stunning views of the city.

Four Seasons Hotel Ritz Lisbon (Lisbon): An upscale hotel known for its classic style, top-notch service, and panoramic views of Lisbon. It features luxurious amenities like a rooftop fitness center, spa, and fine dining options.

The Yeatman Hotel (Porto): A luxury wine-themed hotel in Porto, offering breathtaking views of the Douro River and the city. It boasts a wine cellar, Michelin-starred restaurant, and a spa focused on vinotherapy treatments.

InterContinental Porto - Palacio das Cardosas (Porto): Set in a renovated 18th-century palace, this 5-star hotel blends historic charm with modern comforts. It's conveniently located in the heart of Porto, close to major attractions.

Conrad Algarve (Algarve): A high-end resort in the Algarve region, providing a luxurious beachside experience. The resort offers fine dining, a spa, golf courses, and access to some of Portugal's most beautiful beaches.

Vidago Palace Hotel (Vidago): A grand and historic palace hotel located in the north of Portugal, surrounded by beautiful parklands. The hotel features a spa, golf course, and thermal water treatments.

Martinhal Sagres Beach Family Resort (Sagres): A family-friendly resort in the western Algarve, offering spacious villas and a range of activities for both adults and children, including kids' clubs and water sports.

EPIC SANA Algarve Hotel (Albufeira): A contemporary and stylish 5-star resort with direct access to Praia da Falésia beach. It includes multiple swimming pools, a spa, and an array of restaurants.

Belmond Reid's Palace (Madeira): A historic and iconic hotel perched on a cliff in Funchal, Madeira. This elegant hotel boasts beautiful gardens, stunning sea views, and refined luxury.

Furnas Boutique Hotel Thermal & Spa (Azores): A charming hotel located in São Miguel Island, offering thermal spa experiences and a peaceful setting in the town of Furnas.

Tivoli Carvoeiro Algarve Resort (Carvoeiro): A contemporary beachfront resort with breathtaking views of the Atlantic Ocean, providing a range of leisure facilities and easy access to nearby beaches.

Vila Vita Parc Resort & Spa (Porches): A sprawling luxury resort set within lush gardens overlooking the Atlantic Ocean. It features a variety of restaurants, pools, a spa, and access to a private beach cove.

Please note that the status, facilities, and availability of hotels and resorts can change over time, so it's always a good idea to check their websites or reputable booking platforms for the latest information and reviews before making a reservation. Additionally, some hotels and resorts might offer special discounts or promotions during off-peak seasons, so it's worth looking out for those to maximize your savings. Whether you prefer historic charm, beachfront luxury, or family-friendly amenities, Portugal offers a diverse selection of hotels and resorts to cater to different tastes and preferences.

Guesthouses and B&Bs

As a popular tourist destination, Portugal offers a wide range of guesthouses and bed and breakfasts (B&Bs) for travelers to choose from, stunning its landscape and warm hospitality. These accommodations often provide a more intimate and personalized experience compared to larger hotels. Here's an overview of guesthouses and B&Bs in Portugal:

Charming and Authentic Experiences: Many guesthouses and B&Bs in Portugal are housed in historical buildings, traditional cottages, or old manor houses that have been lovingly restored. Staying in one of these charming establishments allows guests to experience the country's rich cultural heritage and architectural beauty up close.

Warm Hospitality: Portuguese people are known for their friendliness and welcoming nature, and this is evident in the service provided by guesthouses and B&Bs. Hosts often go the extra mile to make guests feel at home, offering personalized recommendations for local attractions, restaurants, and hidden gems to explore.

Beautiful Locations: From the bustling cities like Lisbon and Porto to the tranquil countryside and coastal areas, guesthouses and B&Bs in Portugal can be found in diverse and picturesque locations. Whether you're looking for a serene retreat in the countryside, a beachside escape, or a central city stay, there are plenty of options to suit every preference.

Authentic Cuisine: Many guesthouses and B&Bs in Portugal offer a delicious homemade breakfast with local specialties, providing guests with a taste of traditional Portuguese cuisine. It's not uncommon to find fresh bread, pastries, local cheeses, cured meats, and seasonal fruits as part of the morning spread.

Personalized Service: With a smaller number of rooms compared to larger hotels, guesthouses and B&Bs can provide more personalized attention to their guests. Hosts often take the time to get to know their visitors, ensuring their stay is comfortable and memorable.

Unique Ambiance: Each guesthouse and B&B in Portugal has its own unique ambiance and style, reflecting the tastes and personalities of the owners. Some might focus on a rustic and traditional design, while others offer a contemporary and artistic atmosphere.

Great Value: Guesthouses and B&Bs often provide excellent value for money, as they offer comfortable accommodations, a warm atmosphere, and personalized services at competitive rates.

Here's a list of some popular Guesthouses and Bed and Breakfasts (B&Bs) in Portugal:
Casa Amora - Lisbon: Located in Lisbon, this charming guesthouse offers comfortable rooms and a relaxing garden area for guests to enjoy.

Quinta das Achadas - Porto: Situated in Porto, this B&B features a traditional Portuguese farmhouse setting with picturesque views of the surrounding countryside.

Casas do Porto - Porto: These beautifully restored apartments in Porto provide a cozy and homely atmosphere for travelers.

Monte do Álamo - Alentejo: Nestled in the serene Alentejo region, this guesthouse offers a peaceful escape with stunning rural landscapes.

Casa dos Castelejos - Algarve: This B&B in the Algarve region offers a mix of modern amenities and traditional architecture, giving guests an authentic experience.

Quinta do Scoto - Lisbon: A countryside retreat near Lisbon, Quinta do Scoto provides a tranquil ambiance, perfect for relaxation.

Casa do Valle - Sintra: Situated in the charming town of Sintra, Casa do Valle offers cozy rooms and beautiful views of the area's famous landmarks.

Solar do Castelo - Lisbon: This unique B&B is located within the walls of Lisbon's historic Castelo de São Jorge, offering a memorable stay in the city.

Casa do Rio - Douro Valley: Overlooking the Douro River, this guesthouse provides a splendid setting amidst the picturesque vineyards of the Douro Valley.

Quinta da Palmeira - Madeira: Found on the beautiful island of Madeira, this B&B allows guests to enjoy the lush gardens and a warm, inviting atmosphere.

Casa dos Varais - Azores: Situated in the Azores archipelago, this guesthouse offers a peaceful retreat amid the stunning natural beauty of the islands.

Villa Extramuros - Alentejo: This modern guesthouse in Alentejo offers contemporary design, a refreshing pool, and breathtaking views of the countryside.

When considering a guesthouse or B&B in Portugal, it's advisable to read reviews from previous guests, check the location's proximity to your planned activities, and communicate any specific needs or preferences with the hosts in advance. Whether you're traveling solo, as a couple, or with family and friends, staying at a guesthouse or B&B can add a memorable and authentic touch to your experience in Portugal!

Hostels

Hostels and budget stays are popular accommodation options for travelers looking to explore the world without breaking the bank. They offer affordable prices, communal spaces for socializing, and the opportunity to meet fellow travelers from around the globe. Here's more information about hostels and budget stays:

HOSTELS:

Hostels are lodging establishments that cater primarily to budget travelers. They typically provide dormitory-style accommodations with shared bedrooms and bathrooms, although some hostels also offer private rooms. Here are some key features of hostels:

Affordability: Hostels are known for their cost-effectiveness. Dormitory beds are much cheaper than hotel rooms, making them a great choice for budget-conscious travelers.

Social Atmosphere: Hostels foster a social environment, encouraging guests to interact with one another. Common areas such as lounges, kitchens, and communal spaces are designed to facilitate connections among travelers.

Amenities: Though facilities vary, many hostels offer amenities like free Wi-Fi, laundry facilities, luggage storage, and often have a shared kitchen where guests can cook their meals.

Shared Facilities: In most hostels, bathrooms and showers are shared among several guests in the dormitory. Private rooms with ensuite bathrooms are also available in some hostels for those who prefer more privacy.

Activities and Tours: Some hostels organize social activities, city tours, and outings, providing guests with opportunities to explore the local culture and attractions.

Budget Stays:
In addition to hostels, there are other budget-friendly accommodations that travelers can consider:

Guesthouses: Guesthouses are smaller and more intimate than hotels, often run by local hosts. They offer private rooms with shared or private bathrooms, catering to a more relaxed and homey atmosphere.

B&Bs (Bed and Breakfast): B&Bs provide accommodation with breakfast included in the room rate. They are typically smaller establishments and offer a cozy, personalized experience.

Airbnb: Airbnb is an online platform where individuals rent out their homes, apartments, or spare rooms to travelers. It offers a range of options, from shared rooms to entire properties, allowing travelers to find affordable places to stay.

Hostels with Private Rooms: As mentioned earlier, some hostels offer private rooms alongside dormitory beds. These private rooms often come with the convenience of hostel facilities while providing more privacy.

Here's a list of hostels and budget stays in Portugal. It's always a good idea to double-check the availability and rates before planning your trip.

LISBON:
- Lisbon Lounge Hostel: Located in the heart of Lisbon, offering a friendly atmosphere and budget-friendly dormitory beds.
- Yes! Lisbon Hostel: Centrally located with a rooftop terrace and a social vibe for travelers.
- Home Lisbon Hostel: A cozy hostel with a homely feel, perfect for meeting fellow travelers.

PORTO:
- The Passenger Hostel: A stylish and affordable hostel with a great location in Porto's historic center.
- Tattva Design Hostel: Combining modern design with a budget-friendly approach, offering both dorms and private rooms.
- PILOT Design Hostel & Bar: Trendy and social hostel with a bar, located near Porto's main attractions.

FARO:

- Hostel 33: A welcoming hostel in Faro, close to the city's main sights and public transport.
- Faro Backpackers: A laid-back and budget-friendly hostel with a communal kitchen and a friendly staff.

SINTRA:
- Moon Hill Hostel: Located in the charming town of Sintra, offering a peaceful atmosphere and affordable rates.
- Nice Way Sintra Palace: A cozy and colorful hostel in a historic building, perfect for exploring Sintra's attractions.

LAGOS:
- Olive Hostel Lagos: A budget-friendly option in Lagos, close to the beaches and the vibrant nightlife.
- Rising Cock Hostel: Known for its fun atmosphere and social events, great for meeting other travelers.

COIMBRA:
- Serenata Hostel Coimbra: Situated in the heart of Coimbra, offering a mix of modern comfort and historical charm.
- NS Hostel & Suites: A contemporary hostel with a central location, ideal for budget-conscious travelers.

AVEIRO:
- Aveiro Rossio Hostel: Located near the canals of Aveiro, providing a relaxed stay at an affordable price.
- HI Aveiro - Pousada de Juventude: A part of the Hostelling International network, offering quality budget accommodation.

These are just a few examples of the many hostels and budget stays you can find across Portugal. Whether you're exploring the lively cities or the beautiful coastline, you'll likely find several budget-friendly options to suit your travel preferences. When choosing a hostel, it's essential to read reviews and check the location to ensure it meets your preferences and needs. Booking in advance can also help secure better rates, especially during peak travel seasons. Always consider factors like safety, cleanliness, and proximity to public transportation or attractions when making your decision. Overall, hostels provide a fantastic opportunity for travelers to explore new places, meet interesting people, and create memorable experiences, all while keeping their travel expenses in check. Happy travels!

Travel Itineraries

Portugal is a stunning destination with a rich history, breathtaking landscapes, and a vibrant culture. Whether you're a history buff, a foodie, a beach lover, or an adventurer, Portugal offers something for everyone. Here are three travel itineraries to help you make the most of your visit to this beautiful country:

LISBON AND PORTO DISCOVERY:
Day 1-3: Lisbon
- I Arrived in Lisbon, Portugal's capital city. Spend the first day exploring the historic district of Alfama, where you can wander through narrow streets, visit the São Jorge Castle, and take in stunning views of the city from the Miradouro da Graça.
- On the second day, visit Belém to see the iconic Tower of Belém and the Jerónimos Monastery, both UNESCO World Heritage sites. Don't forget to try the famous Pastéis de Belém, custard tarts that have been made since the 19th century.
- On the third day, immerse yourself in modern Lisbon by visiting places like Parque das Nações, which was the site of the Expo '98, and ride the historic Tram 28 to see more of the city's neighborhoods.

Day 4-6: Porto
- Travel to Porto, Portugal's second-largest city, known for its charming atmosphere and famous port wine. On your first day, explore the historic center, Ribeira, and take a boat tour along the Douro River.

- On the second day, visit the Livraria Lello, one of the most beautiful bookstores in the world, and then head to the São Bento Train Station to admire its stunning azulejo (decorative ceramic tiles) artwork.
- On the third day, take a day trip to the Douro Valley, where you can indulge in wine tasting and enjoy the picturesque vineyard landscapes.

ALGARVE ADVENTURE:
Day 1-3: Far
- Start your Algarve adventure in Faro, the region's capital city. Explore the charming old town, visit the 13th-century Faro Cathedral, and take a boat trip to the Ria Formosa Natural Park to see its diverse birdlife and beautiful lagoons.
- Spend a day at the Praia de Faro, a nearby sandy beach where you can relax and soak up the sun.

Day 4-6: Lagos
- Travel to Lagos, a vibrant coastal town known for its stunning cliffs, caves, and beaches. Take a boat tour to Ponta da Piedade to see the striking rock formations and crystal-clear waters.
- On the second day, explore the historic walls of Lagos and visit the Mercado dos Escravos, which was the first slave market

in Europe. Then head to Dona Ana Beach or Meia Praia for more beach time.
- On the third day, consider a day trip to Sagres to visit the Fortress of Sagres and Cape St. Vincent lighthouse, Europe's southwesternmost point.

CULTURAL IMMERSION IN CENTRAL PORTUGAL:

Day 1-3: Coimbra
- Begin your cultural immersion in Coimbra, home to one of Europe's oldest universities. Explore the historic University of Coimbra, the Joanina Library, and the stunning Sé Velha (Old Cathedral).
- Spend some time strolling along the Mondego River and enjoy the lively atmosphere of the city.

Day 4-6: Óbidos and Sintra
- Travel to the charming medieval town of Óbidos, surrounded by fortified walls. Walk through its narrow streets, visit the castle, and try the famous Ginja liqueur served in chocolate cups.
- On the second day, head to Sintra, a fairytale-like town filled with palaces and gardens. Visit the Pena Palace, Quinta da Regaleira, and the Moorish Castle.

- On the third day, relax at the nearby beaches of Cascais or Guincho before returning to Lisbon or your departure point.

Enjoy your journey through this captivating country!

One Week Adventure

Day 1: Arrival in Lisbon
Your one-week adventure in Portugal begins with your arrival in Lisbon, the vibrant capital city. Check into your accommodation, and spend the afternoon exploring the historic neighborhoods of Alfama and Baixa. Marvel at the colorful buildings, indulge in local cuisine at a traditional tasca, and enjoy a Fado music performance for a taste of Portugal's soulful culture.

Day 2: Surfing in Ericeira
Head to Ericeira, a charming coastal town renowned for its excellent surfing conditions. Whether you're a seasoned surfer or a beginner, there are surfing schools that cater to all levels. Spend the day riding the waves, relaxing on the sandy beaches, and savoring the freshest seafood in one of the local restaurants.

Day 3: Hiking in Sintra
Embark on a day trip to Sintra, a fairy-tale town dotted with castles and lush forests. Explore the

Pena Palace, a UNESCO World Heritage site perched on a hilltop, and enjoy the breathtaking views of the surrounding countryside. Afterward, hike through the mystical woods to discover the hidden gem of Quinta da Regaleira, a mystical estate with intricate gardens, caves, and underground tunnels.

Day 4: Canyoning in Peneda-Gerês National Park
Travel to Peneda-Gerês National Park in the northern part of Portugal, a paradise for nature lovers and adventure seekers. Join a canyoning tour and descend through narrow gorges, abseil down waterfalls, and jump into crystal-clear pools. The rugged landscapes and pristine nature of the park will leave you in awe.

Day 5: Wine Tasting in Douro Valley
Head to the Douro Valley, a picturesque wine region famous for its terraced vineyards and delicious port wine. Take a scenic boat cruise along the Douro River, passing by the vineyards, and visit some of the renowned wineries to indulge in wine tastings and learn about the wine-making process.

Day 6: Rock Climbing in Cascais
Return to the coastal region, this time to Cascais, a charming town known for its beautiful beaches and cliffs. Join a rock climbing expedition along the stunning coastline, experiencing the thrill of scaling

the cliffs and enjoying breathtaking views of the Atlantic Ocean.

Day 7: Kayaking in the Algarve
Finish your one-week adventure in Portugal with a trip to the Algarve, Portugal's southernmost region with stunning beaches and dramatic cliffs. Go on a kayaking tour along the coastline, exploring hidden sea caves and tranquil coves. End your day with a relaxing beach session, basking in the warm sun and reflecting on your unforgettable adventure in Portugal.

Portugal offers a diverse range of activities and attractions, ensuring you'll have a memorable and exciting adventure no matter how you choose to spend your week. Enjoy your trip!

Two Weeks in the Heart of Portugal

Day 1-3: Exploring Lisbon
Your two-week adventure in Portugal begins in its vibrant capital, Lisbon. Arrive at Lisbon Portela Airport and immerse yourself in the city's rich history, picturesque neighborhoods, and delightful cuisine. Start by visiting the historic district of Alfama, with its narrow streets, colorful houses, and stunning views from the São Jorge Castle. Discover the iconic Belém Tower and Jerónimos Monastery,

both UNESCO World Heritage sites, reflecting Portugal's maritime past.

Day 4-5: Porto and the Douro Valley
Take a train or fly to the enchanting city of Porto, famous for its port wine and medieval architecture. Wander through the old town, Ribeira, a UNESCO World Heritage site, and cross the iconic Dom Luís I Bridge, offering breathtaking views of the Douro River. Sample port wine at one of the many cellars that line the riverbank. For a unique experience, take a boat cruise along the Douro Valley, where terraced vineyards and charming villages create a mesmerizing landscape.

Day 6-7: Coimbra and Aveiro
Head south to Coimbra, home to one of Europe's oldest universities. Explore the ancient campus and its stunning Joanina Library. Stroll through the historic center, where cobbled streets lead you to picturesque squares and lively cafes. Continue your journey to Aveiro, often referred to as the "Venice of Portugal." Here, you can take a leisurely boat tour through the city's scenic canals and indulge in traditional sweets known as " moles."

Day 8-10: The Algarve Region
Fly to Faro, the gateway to the Algarve, Portugal's southernmost region known for its breathtaking cliffs, sandy beaches, and warm Mediterranean climate. Spend your time relaxing on the golden

shores or exploring coastal caves and grottoes by boat. Visit the charming towns of Lagos, Albufeira, and Tavira, each offering its own unique charm and history. Don't miss a chance to try fresh seafood and the region's famous cataplana dish.

Day 11-13: Sintra and Cascais
Travel back north to Sintra, a fairytale-like town nestled among lush hills. Marvel at the colorful Pena Palace, a UNESCO World Heritage site, and explore the mystic Quinta da Regaleira with its secret tunnels and gardens. Don't forget to taste the local (pastries) before heading to Cascais, a coastal gem with beautiful beaches and a vibrant atmosphere. Enjoy the stunning sunset over the Atlantic Ocean and savor some fresh seafood in one of the town's restaurants.

Day 14: Return to Lisbon and Departure
End your two-week journey where it all began - in Lisbon. Use this last day to visit any attractions you might have missed earlier or to simply relax and soak up the city's lively ambiance. Sample some of Portugal's finest wines and cuisine one last time before bidding farewell to this wonderful country.

Portugal's two weeks itinerary offers an incredible blend of history, culture, and natural beauty, providing an unforgettable experience that will leave you longing to return and explore even more of this fascinating country. Whether you're a history enthusiast, a food lover, a nature admirer, or all of the above, Portugal has something special to offer every traveler.

Exploring the Algarve Coast

Nestled in the southernmost region of Portugal, the Algarve Coast beckons travelers with its pristine beaches, dramatic cliffs, and charming coastal towns. Renowned for its stunning landscapes, warm climate, and rich cultural heritage, the Algarve Coast has become a favorite destination for adventurers and beachgoers alike. Embarking on a journey along this breathtaking coastline promises an unforgettable experience filled with beauty, excitement, and relaxation.

Beginning the exploration in the vibrant city of Faro, visitors are greeted with a captivating mix of modernity and history. The ancient walls of Faro's Old Town whisper tales of its Moorish past, and strolling through the narrow cobblestone streets reveals quaint cafes, shops, and a sense of the area's distinct charm. Don't forget to visit the impressive Faro Cathedral and take in the panoramic views from its tower. From Faro, a leisurely drive westward leads to Ria Formosa Natural Park, a sprawling network of lagoons and marshlands that is home to a variety of bird species and wildlife.

Continuing along the coast, the journey takes travelers to the picturesque town of Lagos. Framed by golden cliffs and azure waters, Lagos boasts some of the Algarve's most stunning beaches, such as Praia Dona Ana and Praia do Camilo. The famous Ponta da Piedade offers breathtaking panoramic views of natural rock formations sculpted by the relentless forces of the sea. Adventurers can choose to explore these unique geological wonders by taking a boat tour through the sea caves and grottoes.

For a taste of authentic Portuguese culture, a stop in the charming fishing village of Alvor is a must. Alvor's narrow streets are lined with whitewashed houses, traditional seafood restaurants, and lively bars. Wander along the harbor as local fishermen bring in their daily catch, or savor fresh seafood dishes prepared with time-honored recipes passed down through generations

The Algarve Coast is also a paradise for nature lovers and hikers. Head to the Serra de Monchique mountain range, where dense forests and natural springs provide an idyllic setting for exploration. The Foia peak, the highest point in the Algarve, rewards trekkers with stunning vistas stretching across the coast and countryside.

For those seeking a bit of luxury and relaxation, Vilamoura is a haven of elegance and sophistication. Home to some of the region's most luxurious resorts, Vilamoura offers world-class golf courses, designer shopping, and a vibrant marina where visitors can indulge in fine dining and enjoy sunset cruises along the coast.

No journey along the Algarve Coast would be complete without a visit to the charming town of Tavira. Characterized by its traditional Portuguese architecture, Tavira exudes a timeless beauty. Cross the ancient Roman bridge to explore the town's historic castle, churches, and picturesque gardens. Throughout the Algarve Coast, gastronomic delights await food enthusiasts. Seafood lovers will relish the abundance of fresh catches, while the region's signature dish, Cataplana, a seafood stew, is a must-try. Pair these delicacies with a glass of Vinho Verde or Port wine for a truly authentic dining experience.

As the sun sets over the horizon, painting the sky in a blaze of colors, the Algarve Coast continues to allure with its alluring beauty and warm hospitality. Whether it's reposing in the sun on golden strands, probing into history and culture, or seeking thrills in the great outside, the Algarve Coast promises a trip that leaves a lasting print on every rubberneck fortunate enough to explore its treasures.

Chapter 3: Exploring major cities

Lisbon

Introduction to Lisbon

Lisbon, the stunning capital of Portugal, is a city steeped in history and culture, offering a delightful blend of old-world charm and modern vibrancy. Situated on the banks of the Tagus River, Lisbon's strategic location has played a significant role in its rich maritime heritage.

Lisbon's cultural scene is alive with museums, galleries, and theaters, offering a diverse array of artistic expressions. Visitors can immerse themselves in the country's art and history at the National Museum of Ancient Art or the National Tile Museum, displaying the captivating azulejos, traditional Portuguese ceramic tiles. As the day draws to a close, Lisbon's atmosphere transforms, with the sound of traditional fado music resonating through its narrow alleys. Fado, an emotional and soul-stirring musical genre, captures the essence of Portugal's melancholic spirit, touching the hearts of both locals and visitors alike.

Beyond its historical allure, Lisbon boasts a lively contemporary side. The city has witnessed a flourishing culinary scene, with countless restaurants offering delicious Portuguese cuisine, including the famous pastéis de nata, custard tarts that are a must-try for any food enthusiast.

Additionally, Lisbon's inviting climate, with warm summers and mild winters, makes it an appealing destination year-round for travelers seeking both cultural experiences and leisurely relaxation.

Lisbon's allure lies in its ability to embrace its historical heritage while embracing modernity, captivating visitors with its rich culture, stunning architecture, delectable cuisine, and warm hospitality. Exploring this remarkable city is an experience that leaves an indelible impression on the hearts of all who visit.

Top Tourist Attractions

Belem Tower

Belem Tower, or Torre de Belém in Portuguese, is undoubtedly one of Lisbon's most captivating and renowned attractions. This historic fortress and watchtower are situated on the northern bank of the Tagus River, near the point where it meets the Atlantic Ocean. Built during the early 16th century, Belem Tower stands as a magnificent example of the Manueline architectural style, a unique blend of late Gothic and Moorish influences with maritime motifs, reflecting Portugal's maritime glory during the Age of Discoveries. One of the most captivating aspects of Belem Tower is its unique architectural design. The exterior of the tower is adorned with intricate stonework, featuring maritime symbols, knots, ropes, and carved figures representing mythological and historical characters. The tower's balconies and terraces offer stunning views of the Tagus River and Lisbon's skyline, allowing visitors to immerse themselves in the city's maritime charm. The tower's structure consists of four levels, each serving specific purposes. The ground floor served as the main entrance and storage area, while the second level housed the Governor's Hall, used for official receptions. The third floor accommodated the King's Hall, a more elaborately decorated space for important ceremonies. Finally, the top floor or terrace provided a vantage point for sentinels to keep watch over the river and surrounding areas.

Belem Tower is not the only attraction in the area; it is part of a larger historical and cultural complex in Belem, Lisbon. Adjacent to the tower is the

Discoveries Monument (Padrão dos Descobrimentos), a grand monument commemorating Portugal's Age of Discoveries and its prominent explorers. The nearby Jeronimos Monastery (Mosteiro dos Jerónimos), another architectural masterpiece, is also a must-visit site, showcasing exquisite Manueline design.

Belem Tower in Lisbon stands tall as a top attraction, captivating visitors with its rich history, stunning architecture, and its role as a witness to Portugal's illustrious maritime past. Exploring this remarkable fortress and its surroundings offers a memorable journey back in time and an opportunity to appreciate the legacy of Portugal's exploration and seafaring prowess during the Age of Discoveries.

Jeronimos Monastery

The Jeronimos Monastery, located in Lisbon, Portugal, is undoubtedly one of the country's most captivating and celebrated top attractions. This architectural masterpiece, known as Mosteiro dos Jerónimos in Portuguese, stands as a symbol of Portugal's golden age of exploration and its significant contributions to world history.

Commissioned by King Manuel I in the early 16th century, the Jeronimos Monastery was constructed to honor the Virgin Mary and commemorate the successful voyage of Vasco da Gama to India. The king chose the Order of Saint Jerome, also known as the Hieronymites, to inhabit the monastery, as they were renowned for their dedication to knowledge, science, and navigation. The monastery became a center of spiritual devotion, exploration, and learning during the Age of Discoveries.

The highlight of the monastery's architecture is its awe-inspiring cloister, often referred to as the "Cloister of Perfection." This magnificent two-story cloister showcases a remarkable display of stone tracery, delicate arches, and beautifully sculpted columns. The intricate detailing on each column is a testament to the skill and artistry of the craftsmen of that era. As visitors explore the cloister, they are transported back in time and immersed in the grandeur of Portugal's glorious past.

Within the monastery lies the Church of Santa Maria, an exquisite place of worship and an integral part of the complex. The church's interior is adorned with ornate decorations, including magnificent stained glass windows that cast colorful patterns on the stone surfaces. The high altar is a marvel of craftsmanship, showcasing intricate carvings and religious motifs.

One of the most significant attractions within the Jeronimos Monastery is the tomb of Vasco da Gama, one of Portugal's most celebrated explorers. His final resting place, along with other members of the royal family, adds to the historical importance and reverence surrounding the monastery. This extraordinary monument serves as a testament to the nation's golden age of exploration and its enduring cultural legacy, making it a must-visit destination for those seeking to immerse themselves in the rich history and heritage of Portugal.

Alfama District

Alfama District, nestled in the heart of Lisbon, Portugal, is a top attraction site that offers a captivating and comprehensive experience to visitors. As the city's oldest neighborhood, Alfama carries an aura of history and charm that sets it apart from other districts, making it a must-visit destination for travelers.

Alfama's roots can be traced back to the Moorish era, and its name is believed to have originated from the Arabic word "al-hamma," meaning fountains or baths. Throughout its long history, the district has witnessed various civilizations, from the Romans to the Visigoths, each leaving behind their architectural and cultural imprints. Wandering through the labyrinthine streets, visitors can encounter well-preserved medieval structures and archaeological remnants, such as the ancient city walls and the iconic Castelo de São Jorge.

Alfama is synonymous with Fado, a soulful and emotive genre of Portuguese music. This melancholic music has deep roots in the district, and numerous "Casas de Fado" (Fado houses) offer intimate performances by talented local musicians. The stirring melodies, accompanied by heartfelt vocals, capture the essence of Portuguese culture, drawing visitors into the captivating world of Fado.

The National Pantheon (Panteão Nacional) is another highlight, a grand 17th-century monument housing the tombs of several important Portuguese figures. The hilly terrain of Alfama allows for stunning viewpoints over Lisbon and the Tagus River. Whether from the castle's ramparts or the quaint Miradouros (viewpoints) scattered throughout the district, visitors are rewarded with breathtaking panoramic vistas that showcase the city's beauty.

Alfama District in Lisbon stands as a top attraction site due to its historical significance, enchanting atmosphere, rich cultural heritage, vibrant street life, and array of landmarks and scenic spots. Whether it's exploring the ancient architecture, indulging in the emotional melodies of Fado music, or simply savoring the local flavors, Alfama offers a comprehensive and unforgettable journey through the heart and soul of Lisbon's past and present.

Vibrant Neighborhoods

Lisbon, the picturesque capital city of Portugal, is renowned for its vibrant neighborhoods that seamlessly blend tradition and modernity. Each district has a distinct personality, offering a unique experience to visitors and locals alike. Let's explore some of the most vibrant neighborhoods in Lisbon:

Alfama: Nestled on the slopes of Lisbon's oldest hill, Alfama is a historic neighborhood exuding charm and character. Narrow cobblestone streets, whitewashed buildings, and traditional Fado music create an enchanting atmosphere. Lose yourself in the maze-like alleys, visit the iconic São Jorge Castle, and enjoy breathtaking views of the city and the Tagus River.

Bairro Alto: Known for its lively nightlife and youthful ambiance, Bairro Alto comes to life after the sun sets. This bohemian district is packed with trendy bars, restaurants, and nightclubs, attracting locals and tourists seeking an unforgettable evening. During the day, Bairro Alto offers a more relaxed vibe, with art galleries, quirky shops, and traditional cafés to explore.

Baixa: As the heart of Lisbon, Baixa is a bustling neighborhood with broad avenues, grand squares, and neoclassical architecture. The vibrant pedestrian streets are lined with shops, restaurants, and cafes, making it an ideal place for shopping and people-watching. Don't miss the impressive Commerce Square (Praça do Comércio) and Rossio Square (Praça Dom Pedro IV) while strolling through Baixa.

Chiado: Nestled between Bairro Alto and Baixa, Chiado is a sophisticated district known for its artistic flair and upscale shopping. This neighborhood boasts a vibrant cultural scene, including theaters, bookstores, and art museums. Café culture thrives here, with historic coffeehouses like A Brasileira attracting intellectuals and writers for centuries.

Belem: Located west of the city center, Belem is rich in history and offers a mix of traditional and modern attractions. The iconic Belem Tower and Jeronimos Monastery, both UNESCO World Heritage Sites, are must-visit landmarks. Sample the famous Pastéis de Belém (custard tarts) at the renowned Antiga Confeitaria de Belém and enjoy leisurely walks along the Tagus River.

Príncipe Real: This upscale neighborhood is known for its chic boutiques, art galleries, and trendy bars. Príncipe Real Garden serves as a relaxing oasis in the midst of the city, and nearby Embaixada offers a unique shopping experience in a beautifully restored 19th-century palace, showcasing Portuguese design and craftsmanship.

Mouraria: This multicultural and authentic district is one of Lisbon's oldest, where different cultures have converged over the centuries. Explore its vibrant streets filled with diverse restaurants and shops, and be sure to visit the Martim Moniz Square, which hosts various events and markets.

Graça: Offering some of the best panoramic views of Lisbon, Graça is a charming residential neighborhood with a local vibe. It features traditional cafés, small shops, and the lovely Graça Church. Don't miss the viewpoint at Miradouro da Graça, a perfect spot to catch the sunset over the city. These are just a few of the vibrant neighborhoods that contribute to Lisbon's allure and appeal. Whether you're captivated by history, drawn to nightlife, or seeking to immerse yourself in local culture, Lisbon's neighborhoods have something special to offer, making it a city that never fails to enchant its visitors.

Culinary Delights

Lisbon's culinary scene is a fascinating fusion of traditional Portuguese flavors, international influences, and innovative gastronomy. From iconic pastries to savory seafood dishes, here's a comprehensive list of culinary delights you must explore when visiting Lisbon:

Pastel de Nata: Let's start with the star of Portuguese pastries – the Pastel de Nata. These creamy custard tarts with flaky pastry and a caramelized top are a symbol of Lisbon. The best-known place to enjoy them is Pastéis de Belém, where the recipe has been kept a well-guarded secret since the 19th century.

Seafood Galore: With Lisbon's proximity to the Atlantic Ocean, seafood is a significant part of the city's cuisine. Grilled sardines, especially during the summer festivals, are a quintessential street food. Bacalhau (salted cod) is another beloved specialty, prepared in various delicious ways.

Caldo Verde: This comforting soup is a classic Portuguese dish made with potatoes, thinly sliced collard greens, and often topped with slices of savory chouriço sausage.

Cozido à Portuguesa: A hearty and flavorful stew that features an assortment of meats (such as beef, pork, chicken, and various sausages), vegetables, and sometimes beans. It's a delicious representation of Portuguese comfort food.

Arroz de Marisco: A delightful seafood rice dish that showcases the bounty of the ocean. It typically includes a variety of shellfish like shrimp, clams, and mussels, cooked in a flavorful tomato-based broth with rice.

Bifana: For a quick and tasty snack, try the Bifana – a simple sandwich made with marinated, thinly sliced pork served in a crusty bread roll.

Chouriço Assado: These grilled Portuguese sausages, often served with bread and olives, are a popular appetizer or snack, especially in traditional taverns.

Mercado da Ribeira: Visit this bustling food market, located near Cais do Sodré, to experience a wide variety of mouthwatering treats. From artisanal cheeses and cured meats to fresh seafood and pastries, it's a food lover's paradise.

Portuguese Cheese and Wine: Indulge in the rich and diverse selection of Portuguese cheeses, ranging from creamy goat cheese to tangy Queijo da Serra. Pair them with regional wines, such as Vinho Verde, Douro reds, or Alentejo's robust offerings.

Fusion and Innovative Cuisine: Lisbon's culinary scene has embraced innovation, and you'll find restaurants that artfully blend traditional Portuguese ingredients with contemporary techniques. These establishments offer exciting and creative dishes that cater to a more adventurous palate.

Ginjinha: Don't miss trying this famous cherry liqueur, typically served in small chocolate cups, at A Ginjinha, one of Lisbon's oldest taverns.

Petiscos: Similar to Spanish tapas, Petiscos are small dishes perfect for sharing. Try a variety of them to experience the diverse flavors and textures of Portuguese cuisine.

Confeitaria Nacional: Established in 1829, this historic bakery is renowned for its assortment of sweets, cakes, and savory pastries, making it a must-visit for dessert enthusiasts.

Pastel de Bacalhau: This delicious codfish cake, made with salted cod, potatoes, eggs, and parsley, is a popular snack or appetizer, ideal for savoring with a glass of cold beer.

Portuguese Desserts: Besides Pastel de Nata, explore other delightful Portuguese desserts such as Queijadas (cheese pastries), Toucinho do Céu (almond and egg-based cake), and Pão-de-Ló (sponge cake).

Lisbon's culinary delights offer an unforgettable journey through the diverse and flavorful landscape of Portuguese cuisine. From iconic favorites to hidden gems, exploring the food scene in this captivating city is a true delight for every food lover.

Nightlife and Entertainment

Lisbon, the vibrant capital of Portugal, offers a diverse and exciting nightlife and entertainment scene that caters to a wide range of tastes and preferences. Whether you're into music, dance, theater, or simply exploring the city's lively streets, Lisbon has something to offer everyone. Here's a comprehensive overview of the nightlife and entertainment options you can explore in Lisbon:

Bairro Alto: One of the most famous neighborhoods for nightlife, Bairro Alto comes alive after dark with its narrow cobblestone streets filled with a plethora of bars, restaurants, and Fado houses. It's the perfect place to experience a lively pub crawl or enjoy traditional Fado music performances.

Fado Music: Lisbon is renowned for its soulful Fado music, a genre characterized by its emotional and melancholic tunes. Experience an authentic Fado performance at venues like "Clube de Fado," "A Tasca do Chico," or "Sr. Vinho."

Rooftop Bars: Enjoy stunning panoramic views of Lisbon's skyline while sipping cocktails at one of the city's trendy rooftop bars. Popular choices include "Park Bar," "TOPO," and "Sky Bar" at the Tivoli Lisboa Hotel.

Pink Street (Rua Cor-de-Rosa): Located in the Cais do Sodré district, Pink Street is a vibrant hub of nightlife, with its bars, clubs, and restaurants attracting locals and visitors alike.

Casino Lisboa: If you're feeling lucky, head to Casino Lisboa for an evening of gaming, entertainment, and live shows.

Live Music Venues: Lisbon boasts numerous live music venues catering to different music genres. From intimate jazz clubs like "Hot Clube de Portugal" to larger concert spaces like "Coliseu dos Recreios," there's always a show to catch.

Nightclubs: Dance the night away at some of Lisbon's renowned nightclubs, such as "Lux Frágil," known for its electronic and dance music events, and "Main," a popular spot for hip-hop and R&B lovers.

Chapitô: This unique venue is both a circus school and a bar, offering a distinctive experience with stunning views of the city.

Teatro Nacional de São Carlos: For a more cultured evening, attend an opera or ballet performance at Lisbon's historic opera house.

Alfama: The oldest district of Lisbon, Alfama, offers a more traditional experience with cozy bars and restaurants, often featuring live Fado performances.

Cinemas: Movie enthusiasts can enjoy mainstream and independent films at cinemas like "Cinema São Jorge" and "Cinemateca Portuguesa."

Ginjinha Bars: Taste the local cherry liqueur, Ginjinha, at charming bars dedicated to serving this traditional drink.

Night River Cruise: Take a romantic and scenic cruise along the Tagus River, enjoying the beautifully illuminated city landmarks.

Street Performers and Artists: As you explore Lisbon's streets, you'll encounter talented street performers, musicians, and artists adding to the city's vibrant atmosphere.

Themed Parties and Events: Keep an eye out for themed parties and special events happening in various venues across the city, promising a night of fun and excitement.

Remember that Lisbon's nightlife and entertainment scene is dynamic, with new venues and events continuously popping up. Be sure to check local listings, ask for recommendations, and embrace the spontaneous spirit of the city to make the most of your nightlife adventures in Lisbon!

Porto and the North

Exploring Porto

Exploring Porto, the second-largest city in Portugal, is an enriching and captivating experience that unveils a rich tapestry of history, culture, architecture, and gastronomy. Situated along the Douro River in northern Portugal, Porto's unique charm lies in its blend of old-world traditions and contemporary flair. Admire the city's impressive landmarks, such as the Porto Cathedral (Sé do Porto), an imposing Romanesque structure dating back to the 12th century.

Visit São Bento Station, an architectural gem adorned with exquisite azulejo tiles. These beautifully crafted tiles depict significant historical events, offering visitors a glimpse into Portugal's past. Explore the lively Ribeira district, located along the waterfront of the Douro River. Lose yourself in the maze of narrow streets, and soak in the vibrant atmosphere as you encounter street performers, local artisans, and charming cafes. Don't miss the iconic Dom Luís I Bridge, connecting Porto to Vila Nova de Gaia, which offers breathtaking views of the city.

Porto boasts a blend of traditional and contemporary architecture. Don't miss Casa da Música, a modern concert hall designed by renowned architect Rem Koolhaas. Its striking design and exceptional acoustics make it a must-visit for architecture enthusiasts and music lovers alike. Bespeak suckers should explore Livraria Lello, one of the world's most beautiful bookstores. This ornate Art Nouveau gem has inspired notorious authors likeJ.K. Rowling is a true testament to Porto's love for literature and art.

Seek tranquility in the Jardins do Palácio de Cristal, where lush gardens, winding paths, and stunning viewpoints create a peaceful retreat in the heart of the city. Head to Foz do Douro, Porto's upscale beachfront neighborhood, and relish the coastal charm. Enjoy a leisurely walk along the scenic promenade, indulge in seafood delicacies, or simply bask in the beauty of the Atlantic Ocean.

Exploring Porto is a journey through time, where the past gracefully intertwines with the present. From its historic landmarks and breathtaking landscapes to its culinary delights and artistic offerings, Porto is a city that leaves a lasting impression on every traveler lucky enough to discover its treasures.

Port Wine Cellars

Port Wine Cellars in Porto, Portugal, are an integral part of the city's cultural heritage and a significant attraction for wine enthusiasts and tourists alike. Porto, located along the Douro River, is renowned as the birthplace of port wine, and the cellars play a crucial role in the production, aging, and storage of this unique fortified wine.

The port wine cellars are predominantly located across the Douro River from the historic Ribeira district of Porto, specifically in the Vila Nova de Gaia area. This location provides breathtaking views of the city's skyline, with colorful houses cascading down the hillside, and the iconic Dom Luís I Bridge connecting the two riverbanks.

Many renowned port wine houses operate in Vila Nova de Gaia, and most of them offer guided tours and tastings to visitors. During these tours, visitors get a chance to learn about the history of port wine, the winemaking process, and the unique features that distinguish it from other types of wine. The cellars often have vast collections of aging port barrels, giving visitors an insight into the aging process and its impact on the wine's flavor profile.

Port wine is made from grapes grown in the picturesque vineyards of the Douro Valley. After the grapes are harvested, they are crushed and fermented, which is then interrupted by the addition of grape spirits (). This process stops the fermentation, leaving a sweet and strong wine with a higher alcohol content. The wine is then aged in oak barrels for varying lengths of time, contributing to its complexity and taste.

Noble Port Wine Basements Several major and world- famed harborage wine houses operate in Porto, each with its distinct phraseology and flavors. Some of the most notorious basements carry

- **Graham's**: Founded in 1820, Graham's is known for producing rich and full-bodied port wines. Their lodge offers excellent tours and a beautiful terrace overlooking Porto.

- **Taylor's**: One of the oldest port wine houses, dating back to 1692. Taylor's is famous for its elegant and complex vintage ports and picturesque gardens.

- **Sandeman**: Established in 1790, Sandeman is recognizable by the silhouette of "The Don," the iconic caped figure on their labels. They offer informative tours and delightful tastings.
- **Ferreira**: Founded in 1751, Ferreira is renowned for its long history and high-quality ports. Their guided tours provide a glimpse into traditional winemaking techniques.

The Port Wine Cellars in Porto are not only a haven for wine enthusiasts but also a gateway to understanding the region's history, culture, and winemaking heritage. The tours, tastings, and scenic locations make visiting these cellars a memorable experience for anyone exploring the beautiful city of Porto.

Douro Valley

Douro Valley is a picturesque and renowned wine region located in Northern Portugal, along the Douro River. It is one of the oldest and most traditional wine-producing regions in the world, dating back to ancient times. The region is characterized by steep terraced vineyards that line the hillsides along the Douro River, creating a breathtaking and scenic landscape. The Douro River plays a vital role in the region's viticulture, as it not only irrigates the vineyards but also influences the microclimate, ensuring ideal growing conditions for grapevines. The valley's climate is Mediterranean, with hot and dry summers and cold winters. This climate, along with the schist and granite soils, contributes to the unique characteristics of the wines produced in this region. Douro Valley is best known for producing the world-famous Port wine, a fortified wine traditionally enjoyed as a dessert wine. Today, Port wine is produced in a wide range of styles, including Ruby, Tawny, Vintage, and Late Bottled Vintage (LBV), each with its distinct aging process and flavor profile. The Douro Valley is also known for producing high-quality table wines. Since the 1980s, there has been a significant shift in winemaking practices, with a greater focus on producing unfortified wines. These table wines, often referred to as "Douro wines" or "Douro DOC," showcase the region's diverse grape varieties and terroir, resulting in elegant and complex wines appreciated by wine enthusiasts worldwide.

The Douro Valley boasts a rich variety of indigenous grape varieties, each contributing to the region's unique wine offerings. Some of the prominent red grape varieties include Touriga Nacional, Touriga Franca, Tinta Roriz (known as Tempranillo in Spain), Tinta Barroca, and Tinto Cão. For white wines, the region utilizes grape varieties like Gouveio (known as Verdelho), Malvasia Fina, Viosinho, and Rabigato.

Overall, Douro Valley remains a treasure trove for wine enthusiasts and travelers alike, offering a delightful blend of natural beauty, cultural heritage, and world-class wines. Whether you're a wine connoisseur or a curious adventurer, Douro Valley promises an unforgettable experience for all who visit.

Braga and Guimarães

Braga and Guimarães are two historically rich cities located in northern Portugal. They are both significant cultural and historical centers, each with its unique charm and attractions.

Braga: Known as the "City of Archbishops," Braga boasts a long history that dates back to ancient Roman times. It is one of the oldest cities in Portugal and has played a vital role in the country's religious and cultural development. The city is renowned for its numerous churches, ornate cathedrals, and religious festivals.

The Sé de Braga, or Braga Cathedral, is an iconic landmark with impressive architecture and historical importance. The Bom Jesus do Monte sanctuary is another must-visit site, located on a hilltop just outside the city, offering breathtaking views and a stunning Baroque staircase.

Apart from its religious significance, Braga is also a vibrant university town with a youthful atmosphere. The University of Minho attracts students from all over the world and contributes to the city's lively and dynamic character. Braga's historic center is picturesque, with charming streets, plazas, and traditional Portuguese architecture.

Guimarães: Often referred to as the "Cradle of Portugal," Guimarães is recognized as the birthplace of the country's first king, Afonso I of Portugal. The Guimarães Castle stands prominently atop a hill, representing the city's medieval past. The Palace of the Dukes of Braganza is another prominent landmark, showcasing a mix of architectural styles and housing a fascinating museum. Guimarães has a lively cultural scene. The city is known for its traditional festivals, especially during Carnival, where locals don traditional costumes and celebrate with music and dance. The historic center is a delightful area to explore, with cobbled streets, charming squares, and a variety of restaurants and cafes serving delicious Portuguese cuisine.

Both Braga and Guimarães offer a glimpse into Portugal's rich past and provide travelers with an opportunity to immerse themselves in the country's unique history, architecture, and culture. Whether it's the religious fervor of Braga or the medieval charm of Guimarães, these cities are worth a visit for anyone seeking an authentic Portuguese experience.

Central Portugal

Central Portugal is a fascinating region that lies in the heart of the country, encompassing a diverse and captivating landscape. Known for its historical significance, cultural heritage, and natural beauty, Central Portugal offers a wide array of attractions and experiences for travelers.

Geographically, the region is bordered by the Atlantic Ocean to the west, Spain to the east, Northern Portugal to the north, and Lisbon and Southern Portugal to the south. It is composed of several districts, including Coimbra, Aveiro, Leiria, Viseu, Castelo Branco, and Guarda.

Leiria is another significant city in the region, known for its impressive medieval castle perched on a hilltop. The castle offers stunning panoramic views of the surrounding landscape, showcasing the region's picturesque countryside. Furthermore, Leiria is an excellent base for exploring nearby attractions like the stunning Batalha Monastery and the famous pilgrimage site of Fatima.

For nature lovers, Central Portugal offers a variety of outdoor activities. The Serra da Estrela, the highest mountain range in Portugal, is a haven for hikers, skiers, and mountain enthusiasts. Moreover, the region is home to several breathtaking river valleys, such as the Douro and Mondego, providing opportunities for scenic cruises and water-based adventures. Beyond its urban centers and natural wonders, Central Portugal has a rich cultural heritage. Traditional festivals, like the Carnival of Torres Vedras and the Festas de São João in Porto de Mós, showcase the region's vibrant customs and folklore. Additionally, the local cuisine features specialties such as leitão (suckling pig), (salted cod), and moles (sweet egg yolks), which tantalize the taste buds of visitors.

Central Portugal's wine production is also noteworthy, with the Dão and Bairrada wine regions offering tastings of excellent regional wines. Touring vineyards and wineries is a popular activity for those interested in Portugal's viniculture.

Central Portugal is a captivating region that combines history, culture, and natural beauty. Its cities are brimming with historical landmarks and architectural wonders, while its countryside offers diverse landscapes and outdoor activities. Whether exploring ancient universities, strolling along picturesque canals, or indulging in local delicacies, Central Portugal promises an enriching and unforgettable travel experience.

Coimbra: The Ancient University City

Coimbra, known as the Ancient University City, is a historic and charming city located in central Portugal. It holds a significant place in the country's history, as it was once the capital of Portugal before Lisbon. Today, it remains a major cultural and educational hub, primarily due to its prestigious university, which is one of the oldest in Europe.

The history of Coimbra dates back to the Roman era when it was known as Aeminium. Over time, it became a significant city for the Moors and was eventually recaptured by the Christians in the 11th century. In 1290, King Dinis moved the royal court to Coimbra, making it the capital of Portugal until the mid-14th century. The city's rich history is evident in its architecture and historical landmarks. The University of Coimbra, established in 1290, is one of the oldest universities in continuous operation worldwide. It played a crucial role in shaping Portugal's cultural and intellectual heritage. The university's imposing campus, known as "Alta" or "University Hill," is a World Heritage site. Notable alumni include scholars, writers, politicians, and even Portuguese kings.

Coimbra showcases a mix of architectural styles, reflecting its long history. The Alta area features medieval structures, including the stunning Coimbra University buildings, the Old Cathedral (Sé Velha), and the Santa Cruz Monastery. In the Baixa (downtown) area, you'll find elegant 18th-century buildings with beautiful tilework and decorative facades. One of the highlights of the University of Coimbra is the Joanina Library, an opulent 18th-century baroque library. It contains a vast collection of books, manuscripts, and historical documents. The library's architecture, with its intricate woodwork and ornate decoration, is a sight to behold.

Coimbra boasts one of the oldest botanical gardens in Portugal, the Botanical Garden of the University of Coimbra. Founded in the 18th century, the garden offers a peaceful retreat with a diverse collection of plants and trees.

The Mondego River flows through Coimbra, adding to the city's picturesque charm. The riverfront is a popular spot for leisure activities, strolls, and picnics, providing a lovely backdrop to the cityscape.

Coimbra hosts various cultural events and festivals throughout the year. The Festa das Latas and Queima das Fitas, both organized by university students, are among the most famous celebrations that attract locals and tourists alike.

Coimbra is a captivating city, rich in history and culture, with its prestigious university at its heart. Visitors can explore its historical landmarks, enjoy its unique Fado music, and immerse themselves in the academic atmosphere of this charming Ancient University City.

Aveiro: The Venice of Portugal

Aveiro, often referred to as "The Venice of Portugal," is a charming coastal city located in the Central region of Portugal. It is renowned for its picturesque canals, colorful moliceiro boats, and unique architecture, which attracts tourists from all over the world. Here's a comprehensive guide to exploring Aveiro:

One of the main highlights of Aveiro is its network of canals that crisscross the city. These canals were originally built for the transportation of seaweed, known as "," which was used as a natural fertilizer. Nowadays, these canals have become a popular tourist attraction, and the colorful boats offer delightful boat tours, allowing visitors to admire the city's scenic beauty from the water.

The heart of Aveiro lies in its historic center, where you'll find an enchanting blend of traditional Portuguese architecture and Art Nouveau influences. Stroll through the cobblestone streets, and you'll encounter numerous charming squares, historic buildings, and beautiful churches, such as the Aveiro Cathedral and the Church of Mercy.

Just a short distance from the city center, you'll find the stunning Costa Nova Beach. This beach is famous for its unique striped wooden houses, known as "," which serve as traditional fishing houses. The vibrant colors of these houses make for fantastic photo opportunities, and the sandy shores provide a relaxing spot to enjoy the Atlantic Ocean. Aveiro boasts an impressive collection of Art Nouveau architecture. The Art Nouveau Museum is an excellent starting point, providing insight into this artistic movement's history and significance in the city. Walking along the Art Nouveau Route, you'll encounter beautiful facades, ironwork details, and elaborate decorations adorning many buildings.

Aveiro has several museums that offer insights into the city's history, culture, and industries. Don't miss the Museu de Aveiro, housed in a former convent, which showcases religious art and artifacts. The Maritime Museum delves into Aveiro's maritime heritage, while the Museu da Vista Alegre exhibits the renowned Portuguese porcelain and ceramics.

Aveiro's gastronomy is a true delight for food enthusiasts. The city is famous for its delicious seafood dishes, particularly the traditional "Caldeirada de Enguias," a stew made with eels, and the mouthwatering "Ovos Moles," a sweet treat made from egg yolks and sugar wrapped in thin wafer-like casings.

If you're lucky to visit Aveiro during specific times of the year, you might get a chance to experience its vibrant local festivals. The Festas de São Gonçalinho in January and the Festas da Ria in August are particularly lively celebrations filled with music, dancing, and cultural displays.

Exploring Aveiro is a memorable experience, offering a perfect blend of history, culture, nature, and gastronomy. Its tranquil canals, vibrant architecture, and warm hospitality make it a must-visit destination for travelers seeking a unique and charming Portuguese getaway.

Batalha, Alcobaça, and Tomar: Historical Monuments

Batalha

Exploring Batalha and its historical monuments and attractions is a captivating experience that takes you on a journey through Portugal's rich history and architectural splendor. Here's a comprehensive overview of some of the key sites you'll encounter:

Monastery of Batalha (Monastery of Santa Maria da Vitória) This masterpiece of Portuguese Gothic architecture is the crown jewel of Batalha. Its construction began in 1386 to commemorate the victory in the Battle of Aljubarrota. The intricately carved façade, flying buttresses, and exquisite detailing draw visitors into a world of awe-inspiring craftsmanship. The interior boasts stunning chapels, cloisters, and the Founder's Chapel, housing the tombs of King John I and Queen Philippa of Lancaster. The Unfinished Chapels (Capelas Imperfeitas) within the monastery complex showcase remarkable stonework and towering columns, even though they were never completed.

Adjacent to the monastery, the town square is a charming hub of activity. Lined with shops, cafes, and restaurants, it offers a delightful blend of historical ambiance and modern conveniences. It's an ideal spot to relax, enjoy local cuisine, and immerse yourself in the local culture. For a deeper understanding of the town's history and culture, the Batalha Municipal Museum is a must-visit. It showcases a collection of artifacts, documents, and artworks that shed light on Batalha's past, from its medieval origins to more recent times.

Depending on the time of your visit, you might have the chance to participate in local festivals and events that celebrate Batalha's cultural heritage. These festivities often include traditional music, dance, food, and other cultural activities.

Exploring Batalha and its historical monuments and attractions allows you to immerse yourself in Portugal's past and appreciate the architectural, artistic, and cultural achievements of this enchanting town. Whether you're a history enthusiast, an architecture lover, or a traveler seeking unique experiences, Batalha offers a memorable and enriching journey through time.

Alcobaça

Exploring Alcobaça is a fascinating journey through Portugal's history, characterized by its remarkable historical monuments and captivating attractions. Here's an in-depth exploration of the town's key sites:

Alcobaça Monastery (Mosteiro de Alcobaça): This UNESCO World Heritage Site is one of the most impressive Cistercian monasteries in Europe. Founded in 1153, it features a harmonious blend of architectural styles, including

Romanesque, Gothic, and Manueline. The monastery's centerpiece is the Royal Pantheon, where the tombs of King Pedro I and his beloved Inês de Castro stand as a testament to their tragic love story. The kitchen, with its massive chimney and innovative hydraulic system, provides a glimpse into medieval culinary practices.

Church of Santa Maria: Adjacent to the monastery, the Church of Santa Maria showcases stunning Gothic architecture and intricate stone carvings. The rose window on the western façade is a masterpiece, depicting intricate patterns and religious scenes.

Alcobaça Castle: Situated on a hill overlooking the town, Alcobaça Castle dates back to the Moorish period and played a significant role in Portugal's history. While the castle is mostly in ruins, the panoramic views from its grounds offer a unique perspective of the surrounding landscape.

Alcobaça Museum: This museum provides an in-depth look at the town's history and cultural heritage. It features a diverse collection of artifacts, including sculptures, paintings, ceramics, and archaeological finds, offering visitors a deeper understanding of Alcobaça's past.

Cultural Events: Depending on the time of your visit, you might have the opportunity to participate in local cultural events and festivals. These festivities often showcase traditional music, dance, and food, allowing you to engage with the local community and experience authentic Portuguese traditions.

Gastronomic Delights: Indulge in the local cuisine by savoring traditional Portuguese dishes at local restaurants and cafes. Alcobaça is known for its regional specialties, including seafood, pastries, and cheeses.

Exploring Alcobaça's historical monuments, attractions, and cultural offerings provides a deep appreciation for Portugal's past and its rich heritage. From the grandeur of the Alcobaça Monastery to the charm of the local markets, each experience contributes to a memorable and enriching journey through this captivating town.

Tomar

Exploring Tomar is a captivating journey through centuries of history, marked by its exceptional historical monuments and alluring attractions. Here's a comprehensive guide to help you discover the treasures of this charming Portuguese town:

Convent of Christ (Convento de Cristo): A UNESCO World Heritage Site, the Convent of Christ is Tomar's crowning jewel. Built by the Knights Templar in the 12th century and later expanded by the Order of Christ, this architectural marvel boasts a fusion of styles, including Romanesque, Gothic, Manueline, and Renaissance. The Charola, a circular Templar chapel, is a remarkable example of the Order's influence. The Manueline window and intricate detailing throughout the complex make it a must-see. Dominating the town's skyline, the Castle of Tomar is an ancient fortress with origins dating back to the Moorish era. Its strategic location offers panoramic views of the environment. Visitors can explore its walls, towers, and inner courtyards while imagining the castle's historical significance.

Tomar's main square is a vibrant hub lined with charming cafes, shops, and historical buildings. It's a wonderful place to relax, people-watch, and soak in the town's ambiance. The São João Baptist Church, with its ornate façade, stands as a focal point of the square.

Nabão River and Riverside Park: Stroll along the scenic banks of the Nabão River, where you'll find a tranquil riverside park. This area is perfect for a leisurely walk, a picnic, or simply enjoying the serene surroundings.

Portugal's oldest surviving synagogue, the Synagogue of Tomar, offers insight into the town's Jewish heritage. Its well-preserved architecture and museum provide a glimpse into the lives of the Jewish community during medieval times.A unique attraction, this museum showcases an impressive collection of artistic creations made entirely from matchsticks. The intricate sculptures and dioramas crafted from this everyday item are a testament to human creativity.

Albufeira do Castelo de Bode: Just outside Tomar, this reservoir offers opportunities for water-based activities such as boating, fishing, and swimming. The surrounding landscapes of rolling hills and forests provide a tranquil escape from urban life.

Local Cuisine and Gastronomy: Tomar's culinary scene features traditional Portuguese dishes and local specialties. Indulge in regional flavors, including hearty stews, fresh seafood, and delectable pastries like the "Fatias de Tomar."

Exploring Tomar's historical monuments, picturesque landscapes, and cultural treasures offers an enriching experience that unveils Portugal's diverse past and vibrant present. From the grandeur of the Convent of Christ to the peacefulness of the riverside park, each facet of Tomar contributes to an unforgettable journey through history and culture.

Serra da Estrela: The Highest Mountain Range

Exploring Serra da Estrela, the highest mountain range in Portugal, is an enriching and awe-inspiring experience that offers a diverse range of activities for nature lovers, adventurers, and cultural enthusiasts alike. Here, I'll provide comprehensive details about what you can expect when exploring this magnificent destination:

Serra da Estrela spans an area of approximately 1,000 square kilometers and is located in the central part of Portugal. The region is characterized by its rugged terrain, granite rock formations, deep valleys, and pristine lakes. The highest peak, Torre, reaches an elevation of 1,993 meters (6,539 feet) above sea level, providing breathtaking panoramic views of the surrounding landscapes.

Hiking and Trekking:

The mountain range offers a plethora of hiking and trekking trails catering to various levels of difficulty and interests. Some notable trails include:

- **Caminho dos Ganchos:** This trail winds through charming mountain villages, allowing you to immerse yourself in local culture and architecture.
- **Rota das Faias**: A forested trail that takes you through ancient beech trees, offering a tranquil and scenic experience.
- **Rota do Cântaro Magro**: This trail leads to the iconic Cântaro Magro peak, rewarding hikers with stunning vistas.

Flora and Fauna: Serra da Estrela is home to a diverse range of flora and fauna, including endemic species. The high-altitude meadows feature colorful wildflowers during the warmer months, while the glacial valleys are a haven for unique plant species.

Wildlife enthusiasts may encounter animals such as the Iberian ibex, golden eagles, wild boars, and potentially the elusive Iberian wolf.

Queijo Serra da Estrela: No exploration of Serra da Estrela is complete without savoring the famous Queijo Serra da Estrela, a traditional cheese made from sheep's milk. You can visit local cheese producers and learn about the cheese-making process, tasting this delicious delicacy that has become a symbol of the region.

Stargazing:
Serra da Estrela's high altitudes and limited light pollution make it an excellent location for stargazing. The clear night skies provide a unique opportunity to observe constellations, planets, and celestial phenomena. Serra da Estrela is a comprehensive journey that encompasses a variety of activities, from hiking and skiing to immersing yourself in local culture and savoring traditional delicacies. With its breathtaking landscapes, unique flora and fauna, and rich cultural heritage, Serra da Estrela promises an unforgettable adventure for anyone seeking to connect with nature and experience the wonders of Portugal's highest mountain range.

The Alentejo Region

Exploring the Alentejo Region offers a captivating journey through one of Portugal's most enchanting and diverse areas. Known for its vast landscapes, rich cultural heritage, and authentic rural experiences, the Alentejo Region provides travelers with a unique blend of history, cuisine, and natural beauty.

Geographically, the Alentejo stretches across a significant portion of southern Portugal, characterized by rolling plains, vineyards, olive groves, cork oak forests, and charming whitewashed villages. The region is divided into several sub-regions, each with its distinct charm and attractions. The city's historical center is a labyrinth of cobbled streets, Gothic cathedrals, and medieval walls.

Alentejo's cuisine is a delightful reflection of its rural roots. Traditional dishes include hearty stews like "Cozido à Portuguesa," which combines various meats and vegetables, and "Açorda Alentejana," a savory bread-based soup. Olive oil, cheeses, and cured meats also play a significant role in local gastronomy. Nature lovers will appreciate Alentejo's unspoiled landscapes. The Parque Natural do Sudoeste Alentejano e Costa Vicentina offers stunning coastal vistas, rugged cliffs, and pristine beaches. Inland, the vast Alqueva Lake provides opportunities for water sports and stargazing, as it's home to one of the world's first "Starlight Tourism Destinations..

Exploring the Alentejo Region is a captivating journey through history, culture, and nature. Whether you're wandering through ancient cities, savoring local cuisine, or basking in the tranquility of its landscapes, the Alentejo offers an authentic and enriching travel experience that lingers in the hearts of those who venture there.

Évora: A UNESCO Heritage City

Évora, a captivating UNESCO World Heritage City located in the Alentejo region of Portugal, is a treasure trove of history, culture, and architectural marvels. Its well-preserved medieval streets, grand monuments, and unique attractions offer visitors a captivating journey through time.

Roman Temple of Évora (Templo Romano): A true testament to the city's ancient heritage, this remarkably preserved Roman temple dates back to the 1st century AD. The temple's Corinthian columns and intricate design provide a glimpse into the grandeur of Roman architecture.

Cathedral of Évora (Sé Catedral de Évora): This imposing Gothic cathedral stands as one of the city's most prominent landmarks. Its impressive facade, intricate chapels, and stunning views from the tower make it a must-visit site.

Chapel of Bones (Capela dos Ossos): A unique and somewhat eerie attraction, the Chapel of Bones is adorned with human skulls and bones, serving as a somber reminder of the transience of life. The chapel's macabre interior is a thought-provoking experience.

Évora University: Founded in the 16th century, the University of Évora boasts stunning architecture and a rich history. Its grand courtyard and beautiful library offer a glimpse into the academic and cultural heritage of the city.

Giraldo Square (Praça do Giraldo): The bustling heart of Évora, Giraldo Square is surrounded by charming cafes, restaurants, and shops. It's a great place to relax, people-watch, and soak in the vibrant atmosphere.

Évora Museum (Museu de Évora): Housed in a former palace, this museum offers a diverse collection of artifacts, artworks, and historical items that span various periods, providing insight into the city's past.

Almendres Cromlech: Located just outside Évora, this ancient stone circle is one of the largest and most significant megalithic complexes in Europe. It offers a glimpse into prehistoric times and the rituals of the past.

Royal Palace of Évora (Palácio Real de Évora): Though much of it is now in ruins, the Royal Palace offers a glimpse into the opulent lifestyle of Portuguese royalty. The palace gardens are a tranquil oasis within the city.

Aqueduct of Silver Water (Aqueduto da Água de Prata): This remarkable aqueduct stands as a testament to engineering ingenuity. Stretching across the countryside, it once brought water to the city and is now an impressive historical structure.

Igreja de São Francisco: This church is known for its intricate Baroque architecture and the mesmerizing Capela dos Ossos, or Chapel of Bones, located within its premises.

Évora's Cuisine and Wine: Exploring Évora also means savoring its delectable cuisine. Indulge in traditional Alentejo dishes like açorda, migas, and pork-based delicacies. Don't forget to pair your meal with local wines, as the region is renowned for its vineyards.

Exploring Évora is like stepping back in time, as its cobbled streets, ancient structures, and vibrant culture create an immersive experience that captures the essence of Portugal's rich history. Whether you're fascinated by Roman architecture, intrigued by medieval history, or simply seeking a charming and unique destination, Évora has something to offer every traveler.

Beja and Serpa: Off the Beaten Path

Exploring Beja and Serpa: Off the Beaten Path offers a unique opportunity to delve into the rich history, culture, and natural beauty of these charming Portuguese towns. Located in the Alentejo region, both Beja and Serpa are often overlooked by tourists, making them perfect destinations for those seeking an authentic and less crowded experience.

Beja

Castle of Beja: This imposing medieval castle offers stunning panoramic views of the town and surrounding landscape. Its well-preserved walls and towers reflect the area's historical significance.

Regional Museum: Housed in a former convent, the museum showcases artifacts from various periods, including Roman, Moorish, and medieval. It provides insights into the region's diverse history.

Convent of Nossa Senhora da Conceição: A beautiful example of Manueline architecture, this former convent features intricate detailing and a serene courtyard.

Pax Julia Archaeological Site: Unearth the remnants of a Roman villa, complete with mosaics, baths, and other intriguing structures that provide a glimpse into Roman life.

Serpa:
Serpa Castle: Dominating the town's skyline, this medieval castle offers captivating views and a journey through time. The adjacent Serpa Archaeological Museum adds depth to the castle's history.

Church of Santa Maria: This church's Gothic and Renaissance architecture houses impressive altars, sculptures, and tiles that illustrate the town's artistic heritage.

Moura Gate: An ancient gateway to the town, the Moura Gate showcases Moorish influence and leads to charming streets lined with white houses.

Serpa's Walls and Gates: Walk along the well-preserved walls and discover the Gates of Beja, Évora, and Albufeira, each offering insights into the town's past.

Both Beja and Serpa also offer delightful local cuisine, showcasing Alentejo's treasures such as hearty stews, olive oil, local cheeses, and regional wines. The tranquility of these towns provides an excellent backdrop for exploring their unique markets, boutique shops, and interacting with friendly locals.

When visiting Beja and Serpa, you'll find an escape from the more popular tourist destinations, allowing you to immerse yourself in Portugal's authentic culture, history, and beauty. Whether you're captivated by medieval architecture, fascinated by archaeological treasures, or simply seeking a peaceful retreat, these off-the-beaten-path towns have much to offer.

Cork and Wine Country

The Cork and Wine Country in the Alentejo Region of Portugal is a captivating destination that combines the natural beauty of cork oak forests with a flourishing wine culture. This region offers a rich tapestry of experiences, from the sustainable practice of cork production to the artistry of winemaking. Let's explore this in detail and delve into some examples of the diverse wines you can find in the Alentejo:

Cork Production:
The Alentejo's climate and soil create an ideal environment for the growth of cork oak trees. Cork is a sustainable and renewable resource, as the bark can be harvested without harming the tree. The annual cork harvest is a labor-intensive and traditional practice that contributes to the region's

cultural heritage. Visitors to the Cork and Wine Country can witness cork harvesting firsthand, gaining insight into the careful craftsmanship required to transform cork into a wide range of products.

Wine Culture:
Alentejo's Wine Country boasts a vibrant winemaking tradition that dates back centuries. The region's diverse terroirs, characterized by rolling hills and unique microclimates, lend themselves to the cultivation of a variety of grape varietals. Indigenous grapes like Trincadeira, Aragonez (Tempranillo), and Antão Vaz thrive here, producing wines with distinctive flavors and aromas. Alentejo winemakers skillfully blend tradition with modern techniques, resulting in wines that capture the essence of the region.

Examples of Alentejo Wines:
Trincadeira-based Red Blend: Trincadeira, also known as Tinta Amarela, is a versatile grape variety that contributes to the creation of bold and elegant red blends. These wines often display notes of dark berries, spices, and a smooth tannic structure. They pair well with hearty dishes and showcase Alentejo's red wine prowess.

Aragonez (Tempranillo) Single Varietal:
Aragonez, a key grape in the region, can produce single varietal wines with red fruit flavors, gentle tannins, and a touch of spiciness. These wines offer a balanced and approachable profile, making them great companions for a range of meals.

Antão Vaz White Wine: Antão Vaz is a distinctive white grape that produces aromatic and refreshing wines. Known for their citrusy and floral notes, Antão Vaz wines are often crisp and vibrant, making them an excellent choice for seafood and lighter fare.

Red Reserva Wine: Alentejo is also known for its prestigious red reserva wines. These are typically crafted from selected grapes and aged in oak barrels, resulting in complex and structured wines with layers of flavors, including dark fruits, vanilla, and spices. They are well-suited for special occasions and showcase the region's commitment to quality.

Rosé Wine: Alentejo's wine diversity extends to rosé wines, which are gaining popularity for their delightful pink hues and refreshing character. These wines often offer fruity notes and a crisp finish, making them perfect for leisurely sipping.

Sweet Wine (Vinho Licoroso): The Alentejo also produces sweet wines, known as "Vinho Licoroso." Made through the addition of grape spirits to arrest fermentation, these wines exhibit rich sweetness and are enjoyed as dessert wines.

The Cork and Wine Country in the Alentejo Region offers a harmonious blend of sustainable cork production and exceptional winemaking. With a range of grape varietals and wine styles, visitors can savor the diverse flavors of Alentejo wines while immersing themselves in the cultural and natural treasures of this enchanting destination.

The Algarve: Sun, Sea, and Sand

Introduction to the Algarve

The Algarve is a picturesque region located in the southernmost part of Portugal. Known for its stunning coastline, golden beaches, and charming fishing villages, the Algarve has become a popular tourist destination. The region boasts a Mediterranean climate with mild winters and hot summers, making it a year-round attraction. The Algarve is rich in history and culture, with influences from various civilizations that have left their mark on the architecture, cuisine, and way of life. Whether you're looking to relax on the beach, explore historic sites, or indulge in delicious seafood dishes, the Algarve offers a diverse range of experiences for visitors to enjoy.

Beaches and Coastal Towns

BEACHES:

The Algarve's coastline is a breathtaking tapestry of pristine beaches, rugged cliffs, and hidden coves that stretch for approximately 150 kilometers along the southern shores of Portugal. Each beach holds its own unique charm and allure, catering to a variety of preferences and activities.

Praia da Rocha: One of the most famous beaches, Praia da Rocha boasts golden sands, dramatic rock formations, and crystal-clear waters. Its vibrant atmosphere, lined with restaurants and bars, offers a lively backdrop for beachgoers.

Praia do Camilo: Accessible via a picturesque wooden staircase, this intimate beach is tucked between towering cliffs. It's clear turquoise waters and rocky alcoves make it a popular spot for snorkeling and swimming.

Praia de Benagil: This beach is famous for its stunning sea cave, the Algar de Benagil, which can be explored by boat or kayak. The beach itself features soft sands and a serene atmosphere.

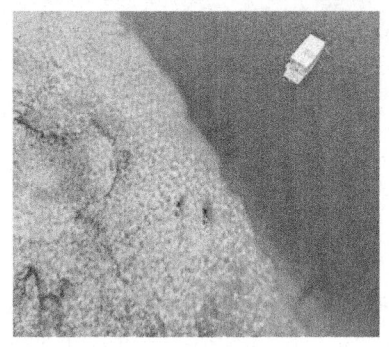

Praia de Dona Ana: Nestled beneath striking ochre cliffs, this beach is known for its colorful rock formations and inviting tide pools, perfect for exploration.

Praia de Marinha: Renowned for its limestone cliffs, sea stacks, and natural arches, Praia de Marinha is often considered one of the most beautiful beaches in Europe.

Praia de Faro: Situated on the sandy barrier island of Ilha de Faro, this beach is easily accessible and offers a lively ambiance with various water sports and beachside bars.

COASTAL TOWNS:

The Algarve is adorned with charming coastal towns that exude a blend of traditional charm and modern amenities. Exploring these towns allows you to immerse yourself in local culture while enjoying the stunning seaside landscapes.

Albufeira: A bustling resort town, Albufeira is known for its lively nightlife, sandy beaches, and charming old town with vibrant markets, restaurants, and entertainment options.

Tavira: Often referred to as the "Venice of the Algarve," Tavira is characterized by its elegant architecture, historic churches, and the romantic Ponte Romana bridge that spans the Gilão River.

Portimão: With its busy marina, seafood restaurants, and waterfront promenade, Portimão offers a vibrant coastal atmosphere. It's also home to the Autódromo Internacional do Algarve, a motorsport racetrack.

The beaches and coastal towns of the Algarve beckon travelers with a harmonious blend of natural beauty, cultural heritage, and recreational opportunities. From the tranquil coves and breathtaking cliffs to the charming towns that offer a gateway to Portuguese culture, the Algarve's coastal paradise promises an unforgettable and enriching experience for every visitor.

Faro and Surroundings

Exploring Faro and its surrounding areas offers a rich tapestry of history, culture, natural beauty, and unique experiences. Situated in the picturesque Algarve region of Portugal, Faro serves as a captivating hub from which to embark on a journey of discovery. Here's a comprehensive guide to help you make the most of your exploration:

Faro Old Town (Cidade Velha): Begin your adventure by immersing yourself in Faro's charming Old Town. Enclosed within centuries-old walls, this area boasts narrow cobblestone streets, historic architecture, and vibrant plazas. The Arco da Vila, a neoclassical arch, serves as a grand entrance to the Old Town and leads you to its enchanting maze of lanes. Explore the Sé Catedral de Faro, an impressive 13th-century cathedral, and the Igreja do Carmo, known for its intriguing bone chapel.

Ria Formosa Natural Park: Just a short distance from Faro lies the breathtaking Ria Formosa Natural Park. This ecologically diverse coastal lagoon system is a haven for nature lovers. Embark on a boat tour to navigate through the intricate network of canals, marshes, and salt pans. The park is a sanctuary for numerous bird species, including flamingos, herons, and avocets. Be sure to explore the barrier islands, where pristine beaches and unique flora await.

Ilha Deserta: As part of Ria Formosa, Ilha Deserta (Deserted Island) is a serene paradise where you can escape the hustle and bustle. Revel in the tranquility of its expansive white sandy beaches and crystal-clear waters. Take leisurely walks along the shoreline, collect seashells, and relish the unspoiled beauty of this secluded island. Enjoy a meal at the renowned "Estaminé" restaurant, savoring delicious seafood dishes.

Ilha da Culatra: Another captivating island within Ria Formosa is Ilha da Culatra. Accessible by boat, this charming fishing village welcomes you with colorful houses, narrow alleyways, and a laid-back ambiance. Explore the local way of life, discover hidden corners, and immerse yourself in the island's unique culture. Don't forget to try some of the freshest seafood in the region.

Tavira: A short drive from Faro, Tavira is a picturesque town characterized by its historic charm and architectural beauty. Cross the elegant Roman bridge that spans the Gilão River and explore the town's cobbled streets. Discover ancient churches, charming squares, and the impressive Tavira Castle. Relax at riverside cafés, sample local cuisine, and soak in the relaxed atmosphere.

Lagos: Venture westward to Lagos, a coastal gem known for its dramatic cliffs, sea caves, and golden beaches. Visit the iconic Ponta da Piedade to witness breathtaking rock formations and panoramic ocean views. Explore Meia Praia, a vast beach perfect for sunbathing and water sports. Discover Lagos' history by visiting the Forte da Ponta da Bandeira and the Mercado dos Escravos, Europe's first slave market.

Sagres: To the southwest of Faro, Sagres offers a rugged, windswept landscape that appeals to adventurers and surfers. Explore the historic Sagres Fortress, which overlooks the vast Atlantic Ocean. The Cabo de São Vicente lighthouse stands proudly as the southwesternmost point of Europe, offering stunning sunsets and a sense of awe-inspiring isolation.

Monchique Mountains: For a change of scenery, venture inland to the Monchique Mountains. Immerse yourself in the region's lush forests, rolling hills, and therapeutic hot springs. Visit the charming village of Monchique, known for its handicrafts and traditional products. Hike to the summit of Foia, the highest point in the Algarve, to enjoy panoramic vistas of the surrounding landscape.

Silves: Unveil the historical treasures of Silves, a town characterized by its Moorish past. Explore the well-preserved Silves Castle, an ancient stronghold with commanding views over the town and countryside. Delve into the region's history and archaeology at the Museu Municipal de Arqueologia.

Culinary Delights: No exploration is complete without savoring the culinary delights of the Algarve. Indulge in fresh seafood dishes, from grilled sardines to succulent prawns. Taste regional specialties like Cataplana, a flavorful seafood stew, and indulge in pastries such as pastéis de nata. Pair your meals with local wines, including Vinho Verde and Algarve's own vintages.

Exploring Faro and its surroundings is a captivating journey that unveils the region's rich history, stunning landscapes, and vibrant culture. Whether you're wandering through historic streets, admiring natural wonders, or indulging in local flavors, this destination offers an unforgettable tapestry of experiences.

Exploring the Rugged West Coast

Exploring the rugged west coast of the Algarve is a captivating and immersive journey that takes you through a diverse landscape of dramatic cliffs, secluded beaches, charming villages, and stunning natural beauty. This region, located on the southwestern tip of Portugal, offers a unique and unforgettable adventure for travelers seeking to experience the untamed and authentic side of the Algarve.

Ponta da Piedade: Start your exploration at Ponta da Piedade, one of the most iconic and photographed spots in the Algarve. This series of sandstone cliffs features intricate rock formations, sea caves, and grottoes that have been sculpted by the powerful forces of wind and water. You can admire the stunning views from the clifftop, or take a boat tour to get up close and personal with the mesmerizing rock formations.

Hiking Trails: The west coast is a paradise for hikers and nature enthusiasts. The Rota Vicentina offers an extensive network of hiking trails that wind through rugged coastal landscapes, picturesque villages, and serene countryside. The Historical Way takes you through traditional villages and historical sites, while the Fishermen's Trail follows the coastline, offering breathtaking ocean views.

Surfing and Water Sports: The rugged west coast is a haven for water sports enthusiasts, particularly surfers. The consistent Atlantic swells create excellent conditions for surfing, and there are numerous surf schools and rental shops in towns like Sagres and Carrapateira. Whether you're a beginner or an experienced surfer, riding the waves of the Algarve's west coast is an adrenaline-pumping experience.

Beaches: Discover hidden and secluded beaches tucked away between the cliffs. Praia do Amado is a popular surf spot with golden sands and powerful waves, while Praia da Bordeira offers a wide stretch of pristine beach bordered by dunes and cliffs. These beaches provide a serene escape where you can relax, swim, or simply soak in the natural beauty.

Cabo de São Vicente: Known as the southwesternmost point of Europe, Cabo de São Vicente is a place of striking beauty and historical significance. The imposing lighthouse stands atop towering cliffs, overlooking the vast expanse of the Atlantic Ocean. Sunset views from this point are especially breathtaking, painting the sky with vibrant hues.

Culinary Delights: Exploring the west coast allows you to savor authentic Portuguese cuisine. Visit local restaurants and taverns to enjoy fresh seafood, traditional dishes like cataplana (seafood stew), and regional wines. Immerse yourself in the local gastronomy to complete your cultural experience.

Accommodations: The west coast offers a range of accommodation options, from cozy guesthouses and boutique hotels to eco-friendly lodges. Many establishments are designed to blend seamlessly with the natural surroundings, enhancing your connection to the rugged landscape.

Exploring the rugged west coast of the Algarve is an exhilarating and enriching adventure that offers a mix of natural wonders, outdoor activities, historical sites, and cultural experiences. Whether you're a nature lover, an adventurer, or simply seeking a tranquil escape, this region beckons with its untamed beauty and authentic charm.

Madeira and the Azores

Madeira and the Azores are both archipelagos located in the Atlantic Ocean, but they belong to different regions and have distinct characteristics. Here's a comprehensive overview of each:

Madeira:

Madeira is an autonomous region of Portugal, situated about 600 miles southwest of Lisbon. It comprises four main islands: Madeira, Porto Santo, and the uninhabited islands of Desertas and Selvagens. The archipelago is known for its stunning natural beauty, mild climate, and lush landscapes. Madeira's landscape is characterized by dramatic cliffs, steep valleys, and terraced hillsides. The climate is subtropical, with mild temperatures year-round due to the influence of the Gulf Stream. This makes it a popular destination for tourists seeking pleasant weather.

Flora and Fauna: The islands are home to a diverse range of plant and animal species, many of which are endemic. The Laurisilva Forest, a UNESCO World Heritage Site, is a prime example of a subtropical rainforest and is found on Madeira. The islands are also known for their colorful flowers, including the famous Madeira orchid.

Culture and Festivals: The people of Madeira have a rich cultural heritage, with influences from Portugal, Africa, and even South America due to historical trade connections. Traditional music, dance, and festivals, such as the Carnival of Madeira, showcase the island's vibrant culture.

Azores:

The Azores is another group of Portuguese islands, situated farther west in the Atlantic Ocean, approximately 850 miles from mainland Portugal. The archipelago consists of nine major islands: São Miguel, Terceira, Faial, Pico, Santa Maria, Graciosa, São Jorge, Flores, and Corvo. The Azores are renowned for their volcanic landscapes and unique ecosystems. The Azores are of volcanic origin, resulting in rugged terrain, hot springs, and even active volcanoes. The climate is characterized by its variability, with frequent changes in weather due to the islands' location within the mid-Atlantic. Despite this, the climate is always mild.

The Azores boast an impressive array of plant and animal species, many of which are also endemic. Marine life, including whales and dolphins, is abundant in the surrounding waters, making the Azores a popular destination for eco-tourism and whale watching.

The Azorean culture reflects its maritime heritage and historic ties to Portugal. Festivals and religious celebrations are an integral part of Azorean life, with events like the Festival of Senhor Santo Cristo dos Milagres on São Miguel being particularly significant.

Both Madeira and the Azores are Portuguese archipelagos with distinct geographical features, climates, cultures, and economies. While Madeira is celebrated for its mild climate, lush landscapes, and floral beauty, the Azores offer volcanic landscapes, marine biodiversity, and a unique blend of traditions.

Madeira Archipelago

Exploring the Madeira Archipelago offers a captivating blend of natural beauty, cultural richness, and outdoor activities. Whether you're an adventure seeker, nature enthusiast, or simply looking for a serene escape, Madeira has something to offer. Here's a comprehensive guide to exploring the Madeira Archipelago:

Lush Landscapes and Scenic Views:
- Madeira's dramatic landscapes include towering cliffs, deep valleys, and terraced hillsides. Exploring these unique terrains can be done through guided hikes or self-guided walks.
- Pico Ruivo, the highest peak on Madeira, offers breathtaking panoramic views. Hiking trails like the PR1 Levada do Caldeirão Verde take you through forests and along water channels.
- The Laurisilva Forest, a World Heritage Site, is a must-visit for its ancient trees, ferns, and mosses.

Levada Walks and Trails:
- Levadas are irrigation channels that crisscross the island, providing a network of scenic trails. These walks range from easy strolls to more challenging hikes, offering close encounters with nature.
- Popular levada walks include Levada do Caldeirão Verde, Levada das 25 Fontes, e Levada do Rei.

Water Sports and Activities:
- The clear Atlantic waters surrounding Madeira are perfect for water sports. Scuba diving and snorkeling allow you to explore marine life and underwater rock formations.

- Whale and dolphin watching tours offer a chance to see these magnificent creatures in their natural habitat.

Adventure and Outdoor Pursuits:
- Adventure enthusiasts can engage in activities such as canyoning, rock climbing, and paragliding, taking advantage of the archipelago's diverse topography.

Botanical Gardens and Floral Wonders:
- The Madeira Botanical Garden and Monte Palace Tropical Garden showcase the island's diverse plant life, including exotic flowers and trees from around the world.
- Don't miss the Madeira Flower Festival held each spring, celebrating the island's floral heritage.

Cultural Experiences:
- Explore the historic city of Funchal, Madeira's capital, known for its charming streets, colorful houses, and historic sites such as Sé Cathedral and the Santa Clara Convent.
- The Mercado dos Lavradores (Farmers' Market) is a sensory delight, offering fresh produce, local crafts, and flowers.
- Engage with local culture by attending traditional festivals, enjoying Madeiran cuisine, and experiencing folk music and dance.

Madeira Wine and Culinary Delights:
- Madeira wine is renowned worldwide. Visit wine cellars to learn about the production process and enjoy tastings.
- Sample local cuisine, which often features seafood, tropical fruits, and traditional dishes like espetada (grilled meat skewers) and bolo do (a type of bread).

Relaxation and Wellness:
- Unwind at natural pools, volcanic sand beaches like Praia Formosa, or luxurious spa resorts.
- The island's tranquil ambiance and mild climate provide an ideal setting for relaxation and wellness retreats.

Exploring the Madeira Archipelago offers a diverse range of activities and experiences, catering to various interests and preferences. Whether you're seeking outdoor adventures, cultural immersion, or simply a peaceful retreat in nature, Madeira's enchanting landscapes and vibrant culture make it a remarkable destination to explore.

Funchal: The Charming Capital

Funchal, the charming capital of Madeira, is a captivating destination that offers a plethora of experiences for travelers to explore. Nestled along the southern coast of the Portuguese island of Madeira, Funchal boasts a unique blend of natural beauty, historical landmarks, cultural attractions, and delightful cuisine. Here's a comprehensive overview of what you can expect when exploring Funchal:

Historic Sites and Landmarks:

History enthusiasts will find a wealth of historic sites in Funchal. The Funchal Cathedral, dating back to the 15th century, is a remarkable example of Portuguese Gothic architecture. The São Tiago Fortress, built to protect the city from pirate attacks, now houses the Contemporary Art Museum. Wander through the streets of the Old Town (Zona Velha) to discover charming cobblestone streets, traditional houses, and vibrant markets.

Cultural Experiences:
Funchal offers a vibrant cultural scene with a range of museums, galleries, and cultural centers. The Madeira Story Centre provides insights into the island's history, while the CR7 Museum celebrates the life and achievements of football superstar Cristiano Ronaldo. Don't miss the chance to witness a traditional Madeiran folklore performance or sample the local music and dance.

Culinary Delights:
Food enthusiasts will be delighted by Funchal's culinary offerings. The Mercado dos Lavradores, or Farmers' Market, is a feast for the senses, with stalls overflowing with fresh produce, spices, and local specialties. Indulge in Madeiran cuisine, which often features fresh seafood, exotic fruits, and unique dishes like "espetada" (grilled meat skewers) and "bolo do " (a type of flatbread).

Outdoor Adventures:
For those seeking adventure, Funchal offers numerous opportunities for outdoor activities. Hiking trails abound in the surrounding hills, leading to breathtaking viewpoints and unique natural formations. The Levada walks, along the ancient irrigation channels, provide a unique way to explore the island's landscapes.

Relaxation and Wellness:
Funchal also caters to those in search of relaxation and wellness. Unwind at luxurious spa resorts, take leisurely strolls along the promenades, or simply bask in the tranquil ambiance of the city's parks and gardens.

Funchal is an enriching experience that combines natural beauty, historical charm, cultural immersion, and a wide array of activities. Whether you're interested in history, nature, food, or simply soaking in the vibrant atmosphere, Funchal has something to offer every type of traveler.

Nature and Outdoor Activities

Madeira:
Madeira, often referred to as the "Pearl of the Atlantic," is a Portuguese archipelago located in the Atlantic Ocean. It is known for its stunning natural beauty, diverse landscapes, and outdoor recreational opportunities.

Hiking and Trekking: Madeira boasts a vast network of well-maintained hiking trails that wind through lush forests, breathtaking cliffs, and charming villages. Some popular trails include the Levada walks, which follow the island's historic irrigation channels, and the challenging hike to Pico Ruivo, the highest peak on the island.

Laurisilva Forests: These ancient laurel forests are a UNESCO World Heritage site and offer a unique and enchanting environment for nature enthusiasts. They are home to a variety of endemic flora and fauna.

Water Sports: The crystal-clear waters surrounding Madeira provide ample opportunities for activities like snorkeling, scuba diving, and surfing. The diverse marine life and underwater volcanic formations make it a diver's paradise.

Whale and Dolphin Watching: The waters off Madeira are a hotspot for spotting various species of whales and dolphins. There are several guided boat tours that offer a chance to witness these majestic creatures in their natural habitat.

Paragliding and Hang Gliding: The island's dramatic cliffs and favorable wind conditions make it an excellent destination for paragliding and hang gliding enthusiasts.

Azores:
The Azores, another Portuguese archipelago, is situated in the North Atlantic Ocean. It is known for its stunning landscapes, volcanic activity, and rich marine life.

Volcanic Landscapes: The Azores are characterized by their volcanic origins, resulting in unique landscapes such as crater lakes, hot springs, and geysers. Sete Cidades on São Miguel Island and Caldeira do Faial on Faial Island are prime examples.

Whale Watching: The Azores are a world-renowned destination for whale and dolphin watching. The deep waters surrounding the islands provide a habitat for many species, making it a fantastic opportunity for marine enthusiasts.

Geothermal Pools: The geothermal activity on the islands has led to the creation of natural thermal pools, such as the ones found in Furnas on São Miguel Island. These pools offer a relaxing and unforgettable experience.

Hiking and Nature Trails: The Azores offer a plethora of hiking trails through diverse landscapes, including lush forests, coastal cliffs, and volcanic craters. The Faial-Pico traverse is a particularly popular multi-day trek.

Caving: Due to its volcanic nature, the Azores have a network of intriguing caves and lava tubes, such as Gruta do Carvão on São Miguel. Guided tours provide an opportunity to explore these geological wonders.

Both Madeira and the Azores offer an array of outdoor activities and natural wonders that cater to a wide range of interests. From hiking and wildlife observation to water sports and geothermal relaxation, these two archipelagos provide unforgettable experiences for nature lovers and adventurers alike.

The Azores Islands

Exploring the Azores Islands offers a captivating blend of natural beauty, unique culture, and outdoor adventures. This archipelago, located in the North Atlantic Ocean, is an autonomous region of Portugal. Here's a comprehensive guide to help you make the most of your Azores adventure:

The Azores consist of nine main islands: São Miguel, Terceira, Pico, Faial, São Jorge, Graciosa, Flores, Corvo, and Santa Maria. Each island boasts distinct landscapes, from lush forests and volcanic craters to dramatic cliffs and pristine beaches. The islands enjoy a mild maritime climate, characterized by relatively consistent temperatures and frequent rainfall. Due to their location, the weather can change quickly, so be prepared for sudden shifts.

The Azores offer an array of hiking trails that wind through stunning landscapes. Notable hikes include the Sete Cidades Caldera on São Miguel, the Algar do Carvão volcanic cave on Terceira, and the summit of Mount Pico, the highest peak in Portugal. Relax in natural geothermal pools, such as the Terra Nostra Park's thermal pool on São Miguel. These warm waters are said to have therapeutic properties and provide a unique bathing experience.

Cultural Experiences:
- **Local Cuisine:** Indulge in Azorean cuisine, which is often influenced by Portuguese, Mediterranean, and North American flavors. Try dishes like das (a stew cooked underground using volcanic heat), lapas (limpets), and local cheeses.
- **Festivals and Traditions**: The Azores have a rich cultural heritage, celebrated through various festivals, processions, and events. Festivals like "Festas do Senhor Santo Cristo dos Milagres" on São Miguel and "Sanjoaninas" on Terceira showcase traditional music, dance, and religious customs.

Practical Tips:
- **Transportation**: You can reach the Azores by air from mainland Portugal, Europe, and North America. Inter-island flights and ferry services provide transportation between the islands.
- **Environmental Conservation:** The Azores place a strong emphasis on preserving their unique ecosystems. Respect nature, follow designated trails, and adhere to eco-friendly practices.

Azores Islands is a captivating journey that will immerse you in stunning landscapes, rich culture, and unforgettable experiences. Whether you're an outdoor enthusiast, a history buff, or a lover of authentic cuisine, these islands have something for everyone.

São Miguel

Exploring São Miguel, the largest and most populous island in the Azores archipelago, is a captivating adventure that showcases the diverse beauty and unique attractions of this volcanic paradise. Here's a comprehensive guide to help you make the most of your visit to São Miguel:

Natural Wonders:
- **Lagoa das Sete Cidades:** This iconic twin lake, one blue and the other green, nestled within a volcanic crater, is one of the most photographed spots on the island. Hike around the rim for panoramic views or kayak on the serene waters.
- **Furnas**: Known for its geothermal activity, Furnas offers attractions like hot springs, bubbling mud pots, and geysers. Don't miss the opportunity to taste " das furnas," a traditional dish cooked underground using volcanic heat.

- **Lagoa do Fogo**: This pristine crater lake is surrounded by lush greenery and offers spectacular vistas. Hike down to its shores or enjoy the view from the viewpoints along the way.
- **Caldeira Velha**: A natural hot spring and waterfall oasis where you can bathe in warm mineral-rich waters amidst tropical vegetation.

Outdoor Adventures:
- **Biking**: Rent a bike to explore the island's scenic coastal roads and picturesque countryside.
- **Whale Watching**: São Miguel is a prime spot for whale watching tours, where you can encounter various species of whales and dolphins in their natural habitat.
- **Surfing**: The island's northern coast provides excellent waves for surfers of all levels.

Cultural and Historical Sites:
- **Ponta Delgada:** The island's capital is a charming city with historic architecture, lively markets, and vibrant streets. Visit the Portas da Cidade and the Sé Cathedral.
- **Tea Plantations:** São Miguel is home to Europe's only tea plantations. Tour the Gorreana and Chá da Gorreana estates to

learn about tea production and sample their organic teas.

Pineapple Plantations: Explore pineapple greenhouses at the Arruda Pineapple Plantation and learn about pineapple cultivation in a unique climate.

Practical Tips:
- **Transportation**: São Miguel has a well-maintained road network, making it easy to explore by rental car. Public transportation is also available.
- **Weather**: Be prepared for rapidly changing weather conditions. Layered clothing and waterproof gear are recommended.
- **Accommodation**:The island offers a range of accommodations, from luxury hotels to guesthouses and boutique inns. It's advisable to book in advance during peak seasons.
- **Responsible Tourism:** Respect local customs, follow marked trails, and adhere to eco-friendly practices to help preserve the island's natural beauty.

São Miguel allows you to immerse yourself in breathtaking landscapes, indulge in local flavors, and experience the warmth of Azorean culture. Whether you're seeking outdoor adventures, cultural experiences, or simply a serene escape, São Miguel has something to offer every traveler.

Terceira

Terceira, one of the Azores Islands, is a captivating destination known for its rich history, vibrant culture, stunning landscapes, and unique attractions. Here's a comprehensive guide to help you delve deeper into the wonders of Terceira:

Historical and Cultural Marvels:

- **Angra do Heroísmo**: The island's main city and UNESCO World Heritage site, Angra do Heroísmo, boasts well-preserved historic architecture, charming streets, and significant landmarks like the Sé Cathedral and São João Baptista Fort. The city's name translates to "Bay of Heroism," reflecting its historical importance.
- **Festivals**: Terceira is famous for its lively festivals. Sanjoaninas, the island's largest festival, features parades, traditional dances, bullfighting, and cultural events celebrating the feast of Saint John the Baptist. Carnival is another colorful celebration that showcases local traditions and creativity.
- **Impérios**: These small, ornate chapels are dedicated to the Holy Spirit and are an integral part of Terceira's religious and cultural identity. They host processions, feasts, and charity events, emphasizing community spirit.

Natural Beauty and Outdoor Adventures:
- **Algar do Carvão:** A remarkable volcanic cave with an underground lake, impressive stalactites, and unique geological formations. Guided tours allow you to explore its mesmerizing interior.
- **Monte Brasil:** A volcanic peninsula that offers hiking trails, historical forts, and panoramic viewpoints overlooking Angra do Heroísmo and the coastline.
- **Serra do Cume**: Visit this breathtaking viewpoint for panoramic vistas of Terceira's patchwork landscape, created by centuries of farming and volcanic activity.
- **Coastal Marvels**: Biscoitos is known for its natural rock pools formed by lava, providing safe and picturesque spots for swimming and relaxation. The striking cliffs and sea arches of Ponta da Serreta are also worth exploring.

Local Cuisine and Delights:
- **Alcatra**: A traditional dish of slow-cooked meat, usually beef, marinated with wine and cooked in clay pots with bacon and sausages. It's a culinary delight that reflects Terceira's Portuguese heritage.
- **Queijadas da Graciosa**: These cheese pastries, originating from the nearby island of Graciosa, are a sweet treat enjoyed on Terceira.

- **Wine and Dairy Products:** Terceira produces its wine, including verdelho, and boasts excellent cheese, milk, and other dairy products due to its fertile volcanic soil.

Practical Tips:
- **Transportation**: Renting a car is recommended for exploring the island's attractions. Public transportation is available but very limited.
- Weather: The climate is mild, but weather conditions can change rapidly. Pack layers and rain gear to be prepared for varying conditions.
- Responsible Tourism: Show respect for local customs, follow marked trails, and practice eco-friendly behavior to help protect Terceira's natural beauty.

Exploring Terceira immerses you in a captivating blend of history, culture, and natural splendor. Whether you're drawn to its festivals, historic sites, outdoor adventures, or culinary delights, Terceira promises an unforgettable and enriching travel experience.

Pico and Faial

Exploring Pico and Faial, two of the Azores Islands, offers a unique blend of natural wonders, volcanic landscapes, and cultural experiences. Here's a comprehensive guide to help you discover the beauty of Pico and Faial:

Pico Island:
- **Montanha do Pico:** The highlight of Pico is its iconic volcanic peak, Montanha do Pico, the highest point in Portugal. Hiking to the summit rewards you with panoramic views of the island and surrounding seas.
- **Vineyards**: Pico is known for its UNESCO-listed vineyards, where unique viticulture practices produce verdelho wine. Visit the historic vineyards, known as "currais," and enjoy wine tastings.
- **Whale Watching:** Pico is a prime spot for whale watching. Embark on boat tours to observe whales, dolphins, and other marine life in their natural habitat.
- Criação Velha: This coastal area features lava rock pools, ideal for swimming, as well as unique lava formations and stunning ocean views.

Faial Island:
- **Caldeira**: Faial boasts its own impressive caldera, Caldeira, a vast volcanic crater. Hike around its rim for breathtaking vistas and explore the lush interior.
- **Horta**: The main town of Faial, Horta, is famous for its marina adorned with colorful murals painted by sailors. Visit the

- **Peter Café** Sport, a historic meeting place for sailors and travelers.
- **Capelinhos Volcano and Interpretation Center**: Learn about the dramatic volcanic eruption of 1957-1958 at the Capelinhos Volcano Interpretation Center, which offers insightful exhibits and a unique lunar-like landscape.
- Marina and Yachting:** Horta's marina is a popular stop for transatlantic sailors, creating a vibrant international atmosphere. It's a great place to enjoy fresh seafood and engage with fellow travelers.

Inter-Island Excursions:
- **Ferry Between Pico and Faial**: A short ferry ride connects these two islands, allowing you to easily explore both. The journey offers splendid views of the surrounding archipelago.
- **Whale and Dolphin Watching Tours**: Both Pico and Faial offer excellent opportunities for marine wildlife encounters, making them ideal bases for embarking on unforgettable boat tours.

Practical Tips:
- Transportation: You can travel between Pico and Facial by ferry or small plane. Renting a car is recommended for exploring the islands' attractions.

- **Accommodation**:Pico and Faial offer a range of accommodations, including hotels, guesthouses, and cozy lodges. Booking in advance during peak seasons is advisable.
- **Responsible Tourism:** Show respect for local customs, follow designated paths, and practice eco-friendly behavior to help preserve the islands' natural beauty.

Pico and Faial allows you to immerse yourself in captivating landscapes, experience local culture, and enjoy memorable encounters with marine life. Whether you're interested in hiking, wine tasting, or simply relaxing by the ocean, these islands provide a remarkable and enriching travel experience.

Chapter 4: Outdoor Adventures

Hiking and Trekking

Hiking and trekking in Portugal offer a diverse and captivating experience for outdoor enthusiasts. The country's varied landscapes, from rugged mountains to coastal cliffs, provide an ideal backdrop for exploring on foot. Here's a comprehensive overview of hiking and trekking opportunities in Portugal:

Terrain and Landscapes: Portugal boasts a rich variety of terrains, making it suitable for both leisurely hikes and challenging treks. The Azores and Madeira archipelagos offer stunning volcanic landscapes and lush greenery, while the mainland features the picturesque Douro Valley, historic Sintra-Cascais Natural Park, and the breathtaking Peneda-Gerês National Park.

Trails and Routes: The country is crisscrossed by numerous hiking trails and trekking routes, catering to all levels of experience and fitness. The Rota Vicentina along the southwestern coast is famous for its dramatic sea cliffs and coastal scenery. The Camino de Santiago also passes through Portugal, offering pilgrims and trekkers a spiritual and cultural journey.

Peneda-Gerês National Park: This UNESCO-listed park in northern Portugal is a paradise for hikers. With a mix of easy to challenging trails, visitors can explore ancient villages, glacial valleys, and pristine lakes. The challenging ascent to the summit of Pico Ruivo is a highlight, rewarding trekkers with panoramic views.

Rota Vicentina: Extending along the Alentejo and Algarve coasts, the Rota Vicentina offers a range of trails, including the Historical Way and Fisherman's Trail. Hikers can relish dramatic coastal vistas, serene beaches, and quaint villages, immersing themselves in local culture.

Sintra-Cascais Natural Park: Close to Lisbon, this park presents a blend of natural beauty and historical sites. Hike through lush forests to discover the enigmatic Quinta da Regaleira and the Moorish Castle. The park's diverse landscapes include woodlands, cliffs, and beaches.

Equipment and Preparation: Proper preparation is key for a successful hike or trek. Make sure to pack appropriate gear, including sturdy footwear, weather-appropriate clothing, a map or GPS device, and sufficient water and snacks. Some trails may require permits, so it's essential to research and plan ahead.

Weather and Seasons: Portugal generally enjoys a Mediterranean climate, with mild winters and hot summers. Coastal regions tend to be more temperate, while mountainous areas can experience colder temperatures and snow in winter. Spring (March to May) and fall (September to November) are popular times for hiking due to pleasant weather and blooming landscapes.

Guided Tours and Safety: For those seeking guidance and local insights, guided hiking tours are available throughout Portugal. These tours often provide transportation, accommodations, and knowledgeable guides who can enhance the experience. Safety should always be a priority – inform someone about your hiking plans, be cautious of changing weather conditions, and stay on designated trails.

Sustainable Practices: As with any outdoor activity, practicing Leave No Trace principles is crucial. Respect the environment, wildlife, and local communities by minimizing your impact, disposing of waste properly, and staying on designated paths. Hiking and trekking in Portugal offer a captivating blend of natural beauty, cultural exploration, and outdoor adventure. With its diverse landscapes, well-maintained trails, and rich history, Portugal is a destination that caters to hikers and trekkers of all levels, promising an unforgettable experience.

Surfing and Watersports

Surfing and watersports in Portugal have become a defining feature of the country's coastal culture and tourism industry. With its diverse coastline, favorable climate, and reliable ocean swells, Portugal has established itself as one of Europe's premier destinations for aquatic enthusiasts. Let's delve into the details of surfing and watersports in Portugal:

Surfing:
- **Top Surfing Spots:** Portugal offers a range of surfing spots catering to different skill levels. Nazaré is world-renowned for its

colossal waves, attracting big wave surfers seeking to conquer record-breaking heights. Ericeira, a World Surfing Reserve, is celebrated for its consistent and high-quality breaks, providing a playground for surfers of all abilities. Peniche, with its famous Supertubos break, is a favorite among competitive surfers due to its challenging and powerful waves.

- **Wave Variety:** The country's exposure to the Atlantic Ocean generates a variety of wave conditions. From mellow beach breaks to challenging reef breaks, Portugal has something to offer for every surfer. The consistent swells and favorable wind patterns contribute to a year-round surf season, making it an attractive destination for both beginners and experts.
- **Surf Schools and Camps**: Portugal boasts numerous surf schools and camps along its coastline, particularly in areas like Ericeira and Lagos. These establishments provide comprehensive surf instruction, equipment rentals, and accommodations for surfers looking to learn or improve their skills.
- **Surf Competitions**: Portugal has gained recognition in the global surfing community for hosting various surf competitions. The World Surf League (WSL) Championship Tour makes a stop in Peniche at the

Supertubos break, attracting top surfers from around the world.

Watersports:
- **Windsurfing and Kitesurfing:** Cascais, situated near Lisbon, is a hotspot for windsurfing and kitesurfing. The Cascais Bay's steady winds and calm waters create ideal conditions for these exhilarating sports. The town has become a hub for windsurfing and kitesurfing enthusiasts, offering rental shops, lessons, and equipment.
- **Kayaking and Paddleboarding**: Lagos, located in the Algarve region, is known for its stunning sea caves, rock formations, and clear waters. This makes it an excellent destination for kayaking and paddleboarding. Tour operators offer guided excursions that allow participants to explore hidden coves and intricate coastline features.
- **Jet Skiing and Wakeboarding**: The Algarve, in general, offers a range of high-energy watersports, including jet skiing and wakeboarding. Tourists seeking an adrenaline rush can enjoy these activities in the region's warm waters and under the sunny skies.
- **Diving and Snorkeling**: Portugal's underwater world is equally captivating. The

Azores archipelago, for instance, provides excellent opportunities for diving and snorkeling. Rich marine life, underwater caves, and shipwrecks create an exciting environment for underwater exploration.

Additional Information:
- **Climate and Accessibility**: Portugal's Mediterranean climate ensures mild temperatures and relatively warm waters, making watersports possible throughout the year. The ease of accessibility, well-maintained infrastructure, and variety of accommodations further enhance the experience for travelers.
- **Local Culture:** Portugal's coastal communities have embraced the surfing and watersports culture. Surf shops, beachfront cafes, and laid-back atmospheres contribute to the vibrant coastal lifestyle.
- **Environmental Conservation**: Portugal places a strong emphasis on eco-friendly tourism and environmental conservation. Many surf schools and watersports operators actively promote sustainability and educate participants about preserving the marine ecosystem.

Portugal's rich and diverse coastline, coupled with its ideal climate and ocean conditions, make it a paradise for surfers and watersports enthusiasts alike. Whether you're a seasoned pro or a novice looking to try something new, Portugal offers a plethora of opportunities to ride the waves and explore its stunning aquatic landscapes.

Cycling Routes

Portugal offers a diverse range of cycling routes that cater to both beginners and experienced cyclists, taking you through stunning landscapes, picturesque villages, and historical sites. Here are some of the notable cycling routes you can explore:
- **Ecovia do Litoral:** This coastal route stretches along the Atlantic Ocean, passing through charming towns, sandy beaches, and rugged cliffs. It offers a relatively easy ride and showcases the natural beauty of the Algarve region.

- **Ecovia do Dão:** Running alongside the Dão River, this route takes you through the lush countryside of central Portugal. You'll ride past vineyards, farmlands, and traditional villages, offering a peaceful and scenic cycling experience.
- **Rota Vicentina**: Known for its dramatic coastal landscapes, this route explores the southwest of Portugal. It consists of two main trails: the Historical Way, which passes through historical towns, and the Fisherman's Trail, which follows the rugged coastline.
- **Cycling in the Douro Valley:** The Douro Valley is famous for its terraced vineyards and wine production. Cycling through this region allows you to soak in breathtaking views of the river, vineyards, and charming quintas (wineries).
- **Lisbon to Porto:** If you're up for a longer adventure, consider cycling between Portugal's two major cities. This route takes you through diverse landscapes, including coastal areas, rural countryside, and historical towns.
- **Alentejo Circuit**: This circular route explores the Alentejo region, known for its vast plains, cork oak forests, and medieval towns. The route provides a mix of challenging terrain and serene countryside.

- **Azores Islands**: For a unique cycling experience, explore the Azores archipelago. Each island offers its own distinct landscapes, from volcanic craters and lush vegetation to coastal roads with stunning ocean views.
- **Madeira Island:** Another island option, Madeira, provides challenging mountainous terrain and spectacular coastal routes. You'll have the chance to cycle through dense forests, quaint villages, and along cliffside roads.
- **Algarve Coast**: The Algarve region offers various cycling routes along its coastline, allowing you to enjoy the sandy beaches, rocky coves, and picturesque fishing villages.
- **Montesinho Natural Park**: Located in the northeast, this park offers rugged landscapes, dense forests, and remote villages. It's a haven for nature enthusiasts seeking a more off-the-beaten-path cycling experience.

Before embarking on any cycling route, make sure to check the router's difficulty level, elevation changes, and road conditions. Portugal's cycling infrastructure has been improving, but it's essential to be prepared with the right gear, maps, and local knowledge. Whether you're looking for leisurely rides or challenging adventures, Portugal has something to offer every cyclist.

Birdwatching and Wildlife Reserves

Birdwatching in Portugal is a popular and rewarding activity due to the country's diverse landscapes, rich ecosystems, and abundant bird species. The combination of coastal areas, wetlands, forests, and mountains provides an ideal habitat for both resident and migratory birds. Some notable birdwatching spots in Portugal include the Algarve region, Ria Formosa Natural Park, the Tagus Estuary, and the Azores archipelago. Bird enthusiasts can spot species like the Iberian Magpie, European Roller, Azure-winged Magpie, and numerous raptors. The spring and autumn seasons are particularly exciting for birdwatching as many migratory species pass through the country.

Birdwatching in Portugal:
Bird Species: Portugal is home to over 600 bird species, making it a paradise for bird enthusiasts. Resident species include the Iberian Magpie, European Robin, Hoopoe, and Eurasian Jay. Migratory birds passing through during spring and autumn include various warblers, swallows, and raptors like the Booted Eagle and the Honey Buzzard.

Birdwatching Hotspots: Several regions in Portugal are renowned for their birdwatching opportunities:

- **Algarve**: The southern region boasts diverse habitats, from coastal areas to wetlands, providing a habitat for a variety of species like the Audouin's Gull and the Kentish Plover.
- **Ria Formosa Natural Park**: This coastal wetland is a crucial resting and feeding place for migratory birds, including flamingos, spoonbills, and herons.
- **Tagus Estuary:** Near Lisbon, this estuary is a Ramsar site, attracting tens of thousands of waterbirds, including the Black-winged Stilt and the Eurasian Wigeon.
- **Azores Archipelago**: This isolated group of islands in the Atlantic Ocean is a hotspot for seabirds, including the Cory's Shearwater and the Monteiro's Storm-petrel.

Conservation Efforts: Portugal has implemented various conservation programs and initiatives to protect its bird populations. These efforts include habitat restoration, monitoring, and raising public awareness about the importance of bird conservation.

Wildlife Reserves in Portugal:
Portugal boasts a range of well-maintained wildlife reserves and protected areas that are dedicated to conserving the country's unique biodiversity. These reserves play a crucial role in preserving various ecosystems and providing a safe haven for native wildlife. Some notable wildlife reserves in Portugal include:

- **Ria Formosa Natural Park:** This unique coastal ecosystem encompasses a series of barrier islands, tidal inlets, and marshes. It's home to a diverse range of bird species, as well as marine life like seahorses and clams.
- **Berlenga Island:** A designated nature reserve, Berlenga Island is a haven for nesting seabirds, including gulls, cormorants, and shearwaters. The surrounding waters are part of a protected marine area, contributing to the island's biodiversity.
- **Peneda-Gerês National Park:** Portugal's only national park covers mountainous terrain and lush valleys. It's inhabited by various mammals, including wild boars, roe deer, and the rare Iberian wolf.
- **Sado Estuary Natural Reserve:** This estuary provides essential feeding and breeding grounds for numerous bird species. It's also a critical habitat for the endangered bottlenose dolphin.

- **Montesinho Natural Park:** Located in the northeast, this park features diverse habitats such as oak forests, meadows, and rocky slopes. It's home to various bird species, including the endangered Spanish imperial eagle.
- **Tejo Internacional Natural Park**: Situated along the Tagus River, this park is known for its dramatic landscapes, including cliffs and river valleys. Bird species such as the Black Stork and the Egyptian Vulture can be spotted here.

These wildlife reserves serve not only as vital habitats for a wide array of flora and fauna but also as educational and recreational destinations for nature enthusiasts, researchers, and tourists interested in experiencing Portugal's natural wonders up close.

Chapter 5: Portuguese Cuisine and Wine

Traditional Dishes to Try

Here are some traditional dishes you should try in Portugal:

1. Bacalhau à Brás - A dish made with salted codfish, eggs, and finely chopped potatoes.
2. Pastéis de Nata - Delicious custard tarts with a crispy pastry crust.
3. Cozido à Portuguesa - A hearty stew made with a variety of meats and vegetables.
4. Francesinha - A Portuguese sandwich with layers of meat and cheese, topped with a spicy sauce.
5. Arroz de Marisco - Seafood rice cooked with a flavorful broth and a mix of shellfish.
6. Caldo Verde - A comforting green soup made with kale, potatoes, and sausage.
7. Amêijoas à Bulhão Pato - Clams cooked with garlic, coriander, and olive oil.
8. Sardinhas Assadas - Grilled sardines, often enjoyed during festivals.
9. Açorda - A bread-based dish with garlic, herbs, and poached eggs.
10. Leitão à Bairrada - Roast suckling pig, a regional delicacy.

These are just a few examples of the many delicious dishes you can savor in Portugal. Enjoy your culinary journey!

Iconic Portuguese Pastries

Portuguese pastries are renowned for their rich flavors, unique textures, and delightful presentations. These sweet treats have become iconic representations of Portugal's culinary heritage and are beloved by locals and visitors alike. Here are some of the most iconic Portuguese pastries that you should definitely try:

Pastéis de Nata: Perhaps the most famous of all, these custard tarts boast a flaky, buttery pastry crust filled with a creamy custard center. Sprinkled with cinnamon and powdered sugar, Pastéis de Nata are best enjoyed warm from the oven.

Queijadas: These small, round pastries are made with fresh cheese, sugar, eggs, and sometimes a hint of citrus zest. They have a delicate, cheesy flavor and a slightly grainy texture.

Travesseiros: Hailing from the town of Sintra, travesseiros are puff pastry rolls filled with almond and egg cream. They are often dusted with powdered sugar and have a distinct almond flavor.

Bola de Berlim:A Portuguese take on the classic Berliner doughnut, these round, fluffy pastries are usually filled with a generous amount of creamy custard or sometimes jam.

Pão de Ló: This sponge cake has a soft, airy texture and is often flavored with lemon or orange zest. It's a simple yet delightful treat that can be enjoyed on its own or as a base for other desserts.

Sonhos: These light and airy fried dough balls are dusted with sugar and sometimes cinnamon. They're commonly enjoyed during festivals and special occasions.

Folhado: These layered pastries can be sweet or savory, with fillings like chocolate, cream, ham, or sausage. The layers of flaky pastry create a satisfying crunch.

Rabanadas: Similar to French toast, rabanadas are bread slices soaked in a mixture of milk and eggs, then fried and coated with sugar and cinnamon.

Ovos Moles: Hailing from the city of Aveiro, these pastries feature a delicate, sweet egg yolk filling enclosed in a thin, translucent pastry shell, often shaped into various decorative forms.

Amêndoas de Páscoa: Commonly associated with Easter, these sugar-coated almonds come in various flavors and colors, making them a festive treat. Each of these iconic Portuguese pastries has its own unique charm and flavor profile, reflecting the country's culinary history and traditions. Exploring the world of Portuguese pastries is a delightful journey that offers a taste of Portugal's cultural and gastronomic richness.

Wine Regions and Tasting Tours

- Portugal is renowned for its rich wine culture and picturesque vineyards spread across various regions. The country offers an array of wine regions and tasting tours that cater to both novice enthusiasts and experienced connoisseurs.
- Absolutely, let's delve into the wine regions and tasting tours in Portugal.
-
- **Wine Regions in Portugal:**
- **Douro Valley**: The crown jewel of Portuguese wine regions, Douro Valley is famous for its terraced vineyards that line the banks of the Douro River. This UNESCO World Heritage site is primarily known for producing Port wine, a fortified

wine that has been celebrated for centuries. In addition to Port, the region also produces excellent red and white table wines. The stunning landscape, with its terraced hillsides and historic wine estates, makes Douro Valley a top destination for wine enthusiasts.

- **Alentejo**: Located in southern Portugal, Alentejo is characterized by its vast plains and Mediterranean climate. It is a diverse wine region producing a wide range of wines, from full-bodied reds to crisp whites. Alentejo is known for its innovative winemaking techniques and commitment to sustainable practices. The region's wineries often offer unique architectural designs and modern facilities that contrast with the traditional surroundings.
- **Vinho Verde**: Translating to "Green Wine," Vinho Verde is situated in the northwest and is celebrated for its young, refreshing, and slightly effervescent white wines. The region's lush green landscape, marked by its proximity to the Atlantic Ocean, contributes to the unique flavors of its wines. Vinho Verde is an excellent option for those seeking a lighter, more aromatic wine experience.
- **Lisbon and Setúbal Peninsula**: These regions are popular for blending cultural exploration with wine tasting. Lisbon's urban

charm pairs well with nearby wineries producing a variety of wines. Setúbal Peninsula is famed for its Muscatel wines and offers not only wine experiences but also stunning ocean views and opportunities for seafood pairing.
- **Madeira**: An autonomous region of Portugal, the island of Madeira is known for its fortified wines that have been enjoyed for centuries. Madeira wine is often used for cooking, but it's also a delightful drink on its own. The island offers unique wine cellars and a chance to explore the production process.
-
- **Wine Tasting Tours:**
-
- **Guided Tours:** Many wineries across Portugal offer guided tours of their estates and production facilities. These tours often include insights into the winemaking

194

process, history, and traditions of the region. Visitors can explore vineyards, cellars, and tasting rooms while learning from knowledgeable guides.
- **Tasting Experiences:** Tasting sessions allow visitors to sample a variety of wines produced by the winery. This is a chance to experience the diversity of Portuguese wines, from the elegant Ports of Douro to the rich reds of Alentejo. Tasting experiences may include food pairings to enhance the flavors of the wines.
- **Harvest Festivals**: Travelers visiting during the grape harvest season (September to October) can participate in vibrant harvest festivals. These events offer a hands-on experience, allowing visitors to join in grape picking and processing activities. It's a wonderful experience to immerse yourself in the winemaking process.
- **Wine and Food Pairing:** Many wine tours in Portugal include food pairing options, showcasing the country's rich culinary heritage. Local dishes are thoughtfully matched with wines to create a harmonious tasting experience that highlights the flavors of both the food and wine.
- **Accommodation in Wineries**: Some wineries offer accommodations, allowing guests to stay overnight in the heart of the vineyards. This provides an immersive

experience, as you wake up surrounded by vines and can even participate in morning activities at the winery.

Overall, Portugal's wine regions and tasting tours offer an incredible array of experiences for wine enthusiasts and travelers seeking to explore the country's cultural and culinary heritage. Whether you're a novice or a seasoned wine connoisseur, there's something captivating for everyone in Portugal's wine country.

Festivals and Cultural Events

Portugal is a country rich in cultural heritage and traditions, which are beautifully showcased through its festivals and cultural events. These celebrations provide a glimpse into the nation's history, religion, and local customs. Here are some notable festivals and events in Portugal:

Carnaval (Carnival): Celebrated in February or March, Carnaval is a lively pre-Lenten festival with vibrant parades, elaborate costumes, and street parties. The city of Loulé in the Algarve region is particularly famous for its extravagant Carnival celebrations.

Fado Music Festivals: Fado, Portugal's traditional soulful music, is celebrated through various festivals such as the Fado Festival in Lisbon. These events showcase performances by renowned Fado artists and provide an immersive experience into Portugal's musical heritage.

Santo António Festivals: Held on June 13th, these festivals celebrate Saint Anthony, the patron saint of Lisbon. The city comes alive with street parties, traditional dances, and delicious grilled sardines. The highlight is the parade of colorful marches through the city's historic neighborhoods.

Festival do Senhor de Matosinhos: Taking place in Matosinhos, this festival in late May or early June combines religious devotion with popular celebrations. It features processions, folk dances, and music, along with the traditional "Fogaças" sweet bread.

Festival of São João: Celebrated on the night of June 23rd, this festival is a nationwide event, but Porto is the epicenter of the celebrations. People hit each other with plastic hammers, release illuminated balloons, and enjoy a festive atmosphere. The tradition of hitting each other with herbs and garlic leeks is also popular.

Feast of the Crosses (Festa das Cruzes): Celebrated in Barcelos, this event combines religious devotion with colorful processions, folk music, and traditional dance. It usually occurs in early May and is known for its intricate flower carpets.

NOS Alive: This is one of Portugal's biggest music festivals, held in Lisbon in July. It features a diverse lineup of international and local artists, spanning various music genres, and draws music enthusiasts from all over.

Feira de São Mateus: One of Europe's oldest fairs, held in Viseu from August to September. It's a vibrant event with entertainment, traditional crafts, food stalls, and a funfair atmosphere.

Festival Internacional de Chocolate (International Chocolate Festival): Taking place in Óbidos, this unique festival celebrates all things chocolate. Visitors can indulge in chocolate sculptures, tastings, workshops, and various chocolate-related activities.

Sintra Music Festival: Held in the enchanting town of Sintra, this classical music festival features performances in historical venues, enhancing the experience with a blend of music and architecture.

These are just a few examples of the many festivals and cultural events that take place throughout Portugal. Each event showcases the country's rich heritage, diverse traditions, and warm hospitality, making them a wonderful way to immerse oneself in Portuguese culture. Keep in mind that specific dates and details may vary from year to year, so it's advisable to check with local sources or tourism websites for the most up-to-date information.

Carnaval and Festas de Lisboa

Carnaval and Festas de Lisboa are two distinct but vibrant celebrations that offer unique insights into Portuguese culture and traditions.

Carnaval:
Carnaval, often referred to as Carnival, is a lively and exuberant festival celebrated in many countries around the world, including Portugal. In Portugal, Carnaval is a time of joyful revelry that typically occurs in February or March, marking the period before the start of Lent in the Christian calendar. It is a time for people to indulge in feasting, dancing, and merrymaking before the more somber and reflective season of Lent.

Key Features of Carnaval in Portugal:
- **Parades and Processions**: Carnaval in Portugal is characterized by elaborate parades featuring colorful floats, extravagant costumes, and lively music. Participants often wear masks and costumes that range from traditional and historical to creative and whimsical.
- **Street Parties**: Cities and towns across Portugal come alive with street parties and

celebrations during Carnaval. Locals and tourists alike join in the festivities, dancing, singing, and enjoying the festive atmosphere.
- **Sátira (Satire) and Social Commentary**: Carnaval provides an opportunity for social commentary and satire. Floats and performances often poke fun at political figures, social issues, and cultural phenomena, allowing for a temporary release of tensions and a chance to reflect on societal matters.
- **Traditional Foods**: Traditional foods are an integral part of Carnival celebrations in Portugal. Sweets like malasadas (fried doughnuts) and (dreams) are commonly enjoyed during this time, adding to the indulgent spirit of the festival.
- **Regional Variations**: While the essence of Carnaval is consistent across Portugal, each region may have its own unique traditions and customs that contribute to the overall festivities. For example, the Carnival celebrations in Loulé in the Algarve region are particularly renowned for their extravagance and creativity.

Festas de Lisboa (Lisbon Festivities):
Festas de Lisboa, or Lisbon Festivities, is an annual series of cultural events and celebrations held in Lisbon, the capital of Portugal, during the

month of June. These festivities are a tribute to the city's patron saint, Saint Anthony (Santo António), and are characterized by a blend of religious devotion, cultural displays, and traditional activities.

Key Features of Festas de Lisboa:
- **Sardine Festival**: One of the most iconic aspects of Festas de Lisboa is the sardine festival, where colorful sardine-shaped decorations and motifs adorn the streets, buildings, and shops of Lisbon. Grilled sardines are a traditional delicacy enjoyed by locals and visitors during the festivities.
- **Marchas Populares**: The Marchas Populares is a grand parade featuring various neighborhoods of Lisbon competing in a display of choreographed dance, music, and costumes. Each neighborhood showcases its unique theme, costumes, and traditional elements, creating a lively and captivating spectacle.
- **Street Parties and Concerts:** The city comes alive with street parties, live music performances, and outdoor concerts. The lively atmosphere extends into the night as people gather to celebrate and dance in the streets.
- **Basilica Celebrations**: Religious ceremonies and processions in honor of Saint Anthony take place at the Sé de Lisboa (Lisbon Cathedral) and the Church

of Saint Anthony. These events offer a glimpse into the religious aspect of the festivities.
- **Cultural Events**: Festas de Lisboa also feature cultural exhibitions, art displays, and theater performances that showcase Lisbon's rich artistic heritage and contemporary creativity.

Both Carnaval and Festas de Lisboa are prime examples of Portugal's dedication to preserving its cultural traditions while embracing modern expressions of festivity. These celebrations provide a unique window into the country's history, creativity, and community spirit, offering locals and visitors alike a chance to partake in unforgettable cultural experiences.

Festa de São João in Porto

The Festa de São João, also known as the Feast of St. John, is a vibrant and exuberant traditional festival celebrated in Porto, Portugal, and other parts of the country on the night of June 23rd to June 24th. This festival is one of Porto's most iconic and eagerly anticipated events, drawing both locals and tourists alike to the city's streets for a night of revelry, music, dancing, and colorful traditions.

The Festa de São João has deep-rooted historical and religious origins, honoring Saint John the

Baptist, the patron saint of Porto. It is believed to have its origins in pagan celebrations that marked the summer solstice. Over time, these festivities merged with the Christian feast day dedicated to St. John, creating a unique blend of religious and secular traditions. One of the most well-known and distinctive customs of the festival is the tradition of "," which involves playfully hitting each other on the head with plastic hammers, often accompanied by humorous or playful greetings. This tradition symbolizes the act of "waking up" to the summer season and is meant to bring good luck.

Food plays a significant role in the celebrations. Grilled sardines, a local delicacy, are a staple of the Festa de São João. Traditional Portuguese dishes such as verde (green soup), (pork sandwiches), and Portuguese pastries are also enjoyed by locals and visitors alike. The streets of Porto come alive with lively street parties, music performances, and dancing. Traditional Portuguese folk music, known as "música popular," is performed, and locals and tourists join in traditional dances. The energetic and joyful atmosphere is infectious, and people of all ages come together to celebrate.

As the night progresses, spectacular fireworks displays light up the sky over the Douro River. Bonfires are also lit along the riverbanks, adding to the magical ambiance of the festivities.

Colorful parades known as "Marchas de São João" wind their way through the streets, featuring elaborately dressed participants, live music, and choreographed dance routines. These parades showcase the artistic and creative talents of the local community.

The Festa de São João is a time for people to come together, strengthen social ties, and celebrate their cultural heritage. It fosters a sense of belonging and unity among Porto's residents and creates lasting memories for both locals and visitors.

The Festa de São João in Porto is a captivating and lively celebration that encapsulates the spirit, traditions, and vibrant culture of the city and its people. It is a time of joy, camaraderie, and shared experiences, making it a truly unforgettable event for all who partake in its festivities.

Folk Festivals in the Countryside

Folk festivals in the Portuguese countryside are vibrant cultural celebrations that reflect the nation's rich history, traditions, and community spirit. These festivals, known as "festas " or "romarias," have been an integral part of Portuguese rural life for centuries, blending religious, agricultural, and social elements into lively gatherings. One of the most iconic folk festivals in Portugal is the "Festa de São João," celebrated on June 23rd and 24th in cities like Porto, Braga, and other rural areas. During this festival, participants engage in playful traditions, such as hitting each other on the head with plastic hammers, releasing illuminated hot air balloons, and enjoying traditional foods and music. In rural regions, especially in the Minho province, locals also celebrate the "Rusgas de São João," where communities come together to sing and dance in colorful processions.

Another significant folk festival is the "Festa dos Tabuleiros" in Tomar, held every four years in July. This event showcases a stunning display of ornate bread trays adorned with flowers, carried by young women in traditional costumes. The festival, with its deep-rooted Catholic origins, combines devotion to the Holy Spirit with joyful communal celebrations.

In August, the "Festa da Senhora da Agonia" in Viana do Castelo draws thousands of visitors. This maritime-themed festival honors the city's patron saint and includes a parade of colorful traditional costumes, decorated boats, and lively street parties. The "Feira de São Mateus" in Viseu, occurring between August and September, is one of Portugal's oldest fairs. Initially an agricultural fair, it has evolved into a vibrant event featuring concerts, amusement rides, artisanal goods, and regional gastronomy, providing a mix of tradition and modernity.

A common thread among these festivals is the fusion of religious and pagan elements, reflecting the deeply ingrained cultural and historical fabric of Portugal. They are characterized by vibrant processions, live music performances, traditional dances like the "Vira," and culinary specialties that showcase local flavors.

These folk festivals hold immense importance in maintaining a sense of community, preserving cultural heritage, and attracting tourists interested in experiencing authentic Portuguese traditions. The sense of unity, pride, and identity that these festivals foster in the countryside is an integral part of Portugal's cultural tapestry, providing an opportunity for locals and visitors alike to immerse themselves in the country's rich history and celebrate its enduring spirit.

Chapter 6: Practical Tips for Travelers

Health and Safety

Health and safety tips in Portugal are essential for a safe and enjoyable experience while traveling or living in the country. Here's a comprehensive guide to help you stay healthy and safe:

1. Medical Care: Portugal has a well-developed healthcare system, but it's recommended to have travel insurance to cover any medical expenses. European Health Insurance Card (EHIC) holders can access state healthcare at reduced rates. Familiarize yourself with local medical facilities and emergency contact numbers.

2. Hygiene: Maintain good personal hygiene, especially during the COVID-19 pandemic. Wash your hands frequently, use hand sanitizers, and follow local health guidelines for wearing masks and social distancing.

3. Vaccinations: Check with your healthcare provider for recommended vaccinations before traveling to Portugal. Ensure that your routine vaccinations are updated.

4. Food and Water: Portugal generally has safe tap water, but bottled water is widely available. Stick to well-cooked and hot foods, and avoid consuming raw or undercooked seafood. Be cautious with street food and choose restaurants with good hygiene practices.

5. Sun Safety: Portugal enjoys a sunny climate, so protect yourself from sunburn by wearing sunscreen, sunglasses, and a hat. Drink a lot of water to stay hydrated, especially during the hot summer months.

6. Beach Safety: If you're planning to swim, pay attention to lifeguard warnings and flags indicating sea conditions. Follow their instructions and be cautious of strong currents and tides.

7. Outdoor Activities: If you're hiking or engaging in outdoor activities, wear appropriate footwear and clothing. Stay on marked trails, and be cautious of wildlife and insects.

8. Emergency Services: The emergency number for police, ambulance, and fire services in Portugal is 112. Save this number and know how to ask for help in Portuguese if needed.

9. Traffic Safety: Portugal has strict traffic rules. Always wear seatbelts, follow speed limits, and avoid using your phone while driving. Use crosswalks when walking and be cautious of traffic.

10. Travel Insurance: It's advisable to have comprehensive travel insurance that covers medical emergencies, trip cancellations, and other unforeseen events.

11. Language: While English is widely spoken in tourist areas, learning a few basic Portuguese phrases can be helpful in communicating with locals and seeking assistance.

12. Cultural Sensitivity: Respect local customs and traditions. Dress modestly when visiting religious sites, and be mindful of local sensitivities.

13. Emergency Preparedness: Familiarize yourself with the layout of your accommodation, locate emergency exits, and have a plan in case of emergencies.

Remember that health and safety recommendations can change over time, so it's a good idea to stay updated with the latest information before and during your visit to Portugal.

Money Matters

Money matters in Portugal encompass a wide range of financial aspects that impact both residents and visitors to the country. From its currency and banking system to taxation, cost of living, and investment opportunities, here's a comprehensive overview:

Currency and Banking System:

The official currency of Portugal is the Euro (€), which is divided into 100 cents. Portugal adopted the Euro in 1999, and it has since become the sole legal tender for all financial transactions. The country has a well-developed banking system, with a mix of domestic and international banks offering a variety of services, including savings accounts, checking accounts, loans, mortgages, and investment options.

Cost of Living:

The cost of living in Portugal can vary significantly based on factors such as location, lifestyle, and personal preferences. Lisbon and Porto, as the major cities, tend to have higher costs of living compared to more rural areas. Housing costs, particularly in urban centers, can be a significant expense. Renting is common, and rental prices have experienced fluctuations in recent years. Other factors contributing to the cost of living include transportation, healthcare, education, utilities, and entertainment.

Real Estate and Housing:

Real estate in Portugal has garnered attention from both domestic and foreign investors. Urban areas, especially Lisbon and Porto, have seen increased demand and property value appreciation. The

Golden Visa program has also attracted real estate investors by offering residency to those who invest a certain amount in Portuguese properties. The rental market is competitive, particularly in urban centers, and short-term rentals have become popular through platforms like Airbnb.

Taxation:

Portugal has a progressive tax system that includes various types of taxes, such as income tax, corporate tax, and value-added tax (VAT). The income tax rates are progressive, ranging from 14.5% to 48%, depending on the income level. The VAT rates vary between standard rates (ranging from 6% to 23%) and reduced rates (ranging from 4% to 13%) for specific goods and services. Portugal also has double taxation treaties with numerous countries to avoid double taxation of income.

Non-Habitual Resident (NHR) Regime:

The NHR regime is a tax incentive aimed at attracting foreign individuals to Portugal. Eligible individuals, including retirees and professionals, can benefit from a 10-year tax exemption on foreign-sourced income, including pensions and certain professional income, provided they meet specific criteria. This regime has contributed to Portugal's appeal as a retirement and expatriate destination.

Investment Opportunities:

Portugal offers diverse investment opportunities, including real estate, tourism, renewable energy, technology, and agriculture. The country has made significant investments in renewable energy projects, particularly wind and solar power. Tourism-related investments have also thrived due to Portugal's attractive landscapes and cultural heritage. Additionally, technology startups have gained momentum, especially in Lisbon and Porto.

Banking and Financial Services:

Portugal's banking sector is well-regulated and includes a mix of traditional brick-and-mortar banks as well as online banking options. Online banking and mobile payment solutions are widely accessible, making financial transactions convenient for residents and visitors alike. The country also has a strong network of ATMs, which accept major international credit and debit cards.

Economic Outlook:

Portugal's economy has experienced periods of growth and recovery in recent years. The country has benefited from tourism, exports, and foreign investment. While economic challenges exist, Portugal's strategic location, infrastructure development, and access to European markets contribute to its overall economic stability.

It's important to stay informed about the latest financial regulations, tax laws, and economic developments in Portugal. Seeking advice from financial professionals and conducting thorough research before making any financial decisions is recommended to ensure a solid understanding of the country's money matters.

Language and Communication

Language and communication in Portugal are deeply rooted in the country's history, culture, and social fabric. Portuguese is the official language of Portugal and serves as a unifying force that binds the diverse regions of the country together. Here's a comprehensive overview of language and communication in Portugal:

Language Identity: Portuguese, often referred to as "Língua Portuguesa," is the native language of Portugal. It has a rich history, dating back to the medieval Galician-Portuguese spoken in the region. The language has evolved over the centuries, influenced by Latin, Arabic, and other languages due to historical interactions.

Language Diversity: While Portuguese is the primary language, there are regional dialects and accents that reflect the country's diverse cultural heritage. Some areas, such as the Azores and Madeira islands, have distinct accents and linguistic features. Mirandese, a local language related to Portuguese, is also recognized as a co-official language in the region of Miranda do Douro.

Colonial Legacy: Portugal's colonial history significantly impacted its language and communication. Portuguese explorers and settlers spread the language to various parts of the world, leading to the creation of Lusophone communities in Africa, Asia, and South America. Countries like Brazil, Mozambique, Angola, and Cape Verde have Portuguese as an official or widely spoken language due to colonization.

Literary Heritage: Portugal has a rich literary tradition that spans centuries. From medieval troubadour poetry to the works of famous poets like Luís de Camões and Fernando Pessoa, Portuguese literature has made significant contributions to world literature. The country's literary heritage is celebrated through various events, festivals, and literary prizes.

Communication Media: Portugal has a well-developed media landscape, encompassing television, radio, print, and digital platforms. Public broadcasting services like RTP (Rádio e Televisão de Portugal) play a crucial role in disseminating information, entertainment, and cultural content. Newspapers and magazines contribute to public discourse and reflection of societal issues.

Cultural Expressions: Language and communication are intertwined with Portugal's cultural expressions. Fado, a traditional genre of music characterized by melancholic themes, often reflects the emotional depth of Portuguese language and storytelling. Other cultural forms like theater, cinema, and visual arts also contribute to the nation's communication landscape.

Education and Language Policies: The Portuguese government emphasizes the importance of language education and preservation. Portuguese is taught in schools as the primary language, and efforts are made to promote literacy and language skills. Additionally, the government supports initiatives to protect and promote regional languages like Mirandese.

Global Interaction: Portugal's engagement in international trade, diplomacy, and cultural exchange has necessitated effective communication in various languages. English is commonly taught as a second language, enabling communication with a global audience and fostering economic and cultural ties.

In conclusion, language and communication in Portugal are dynamic and multifaceted, reflecting the nation's historical legacy, cultural diversity, and global interactions. Portuguese serves as a bridge that connects Portugal to its past, its diaspora, and the wider world, while also facilitating dialogue and expression within the country itself.

Dos and Don'ts

Here's a comprehensive and detailed guide on the Dos and Don'ts in Portugal:

Dos:
Greetings and Etiquette:
- When meeting someone for the first time, ensure a handshake with a kind gesture. Friends and acquaintances often greet each other with a kiss on both cheeks.
- Use polite language such as "Bom dia" (Good morning), "Boa tarde" (Good afternoon), and "Boa " (Good evening) when entering shops, restaurants, or public spaces.
- Address people using their titles (Senhor for Mr. and Senhora for Mrs.) followed by their last name.

Mealtime Etiquette:
- Enjoy Portuguese cuisine, which often includes fish, seafood, and delicious pastries.
- Wait for the host or hostess to start eating before you begin your meal.
- Keep your hands visible on the table while eating, and use utensils for dining.
- Taste a little bit of everything on your plate to show appreciation for the meal.

Dress Code:
- Portugal is relatively relaxed in terms of dress, but in more formal settings and religious places, modest clothing is appreciated.
- In beach areas, swimwear is appropriate only on the beach or at beachside establishments.

Socializing:
- Portuguese people are generally warm and friendly. Engage in conversations, but avoid sensitive topics like politics and religion.
- Show genuine interest in others by asking about their families and well-being.

Tipping:
- Tipping is customary in restaurants and cafes. Leaving a small tip of around 5-10% is appreciated.
- Tip taxi drivers, hotel staff, and tour guides when appropriate.

Cultural Respect:
- When visiting churches or other religious sites, dress properly and behave respectfully.
- Show appreciation for the traditional Fado music by being attentive and clapping after performances.

Language Efforts:
- While many Portuguese people speak English, making an effort to learn basic Portuguese phrases like "Por favor" (please) and "Obrigado/a" (thank you) shows respect for the local culture.

Don'ts:
Punctuality:
- Don't be too early for social events or appointments, as it might inconvenience your hosts.

Loud Behavior:
- Avoid talking loudly in public spaces, as it can be considered disrespectful.

Cultural Sensitivity:
- Don't make negative comments about Portugal or its history, as many Portuguese people are proud of their heritage.
- Refrain from discussing financial matters openly.

Safety and Security:
- Don't leave your belongings unattended in public places, as petty theft can occur, especially in tourist areas.

Respect Siesta Time:
- Don't expect all shops and businesses to be open during the afternoon hours. Many places may close for a siesta break.

Driving Etiquette:
- Avoid aggressive driving and obey traffic rules. Be patient on narrow roads and respect pedestrian crossings.

Over-Tipping:
- While tipping is customary, don't over-tip to the extent that it feels excessive to the locals.

Cultural Misunderstandings:
- Don't assume that all regions of Portugal are the same. Different areas might have distinct customs and traditions.

Public Display of Affection:
- While it's generally acceptable to show affection, avoid excessive public displays of affection, especially in more conservative areas.

Neglecting Planning:
- Don't underestimate distances between cities. Plan your travel and activities with enough time in mind.

Remember, adapting to local customs and etiquette is a sign of respect and will enhance your experience in Portugal. Keep an open mind, be observant, and enjoy the rich culture and traditions the country has to offer.

Responsible Tourism Initiatives

Portugal has been proactive in implementing responsible tourism initiatives to ensure the sustainable development of its tourism industry while preserving its natural and cultural heritage. Here are some comprehensive details about responsible tourism initiatives in Portugal:

Certification Programs: Portugal has introduced various certification programs that encourage sustainable practices among tourism businesses. The "Clean & Safe" certification, launched in response to the COVID-19 pandemic, ensures that tourism establishments follow health and safety protocols. The "Biosphere" certification recognizes businesses that meet strict sustainability criteria, covering aspects like energy efficiency, waste reduction, and community engagement.

Promotion of Eco-Friendly Accommodations: The country promotes eco-friendly accommodations such as eco-resorts, agrotourism farms, and sustainable lodges. These establishments often focus on minimizing their environmental impact, using renewable energy sources, managing waste responsibly, and promoting local and organic produce.

Wildlife and Nature Conservation: Portugal places a strong emphasis on protecting its unique ecosystems and wildlife. Initiatives like the "Dolphin Watching Guidelines" provide guidelines for responsible wildlife watching, ensuring that tourism activities do not disturb or harm marine life.

Cultural Preservation: Responsible tourism initiatives in Portugal also prioritize the preservation of cultural heritage. Museums, historical sites, and local communities are engaged in efforts to conserve traditional practices, architecture, and customs, allowing tourists to experience authentic Portuguese culture.

Sustainable Transportation: The country encourages sustainable transportation options for tourists. Bike-sharing programs, electric vehicle charging stations, and improved public transportation infrastructure make it easier for visitors to explore without relying solely on cars.

Waste Management and Reduction: Portugal promotes waste reduction and recycling in the tourism sector. Many tourist areas have implemented recycling programs, and some hotels and restaurants have adopted zero-waste practices, reducing their environmental footprint.

Local Community Involvement: Responsible tourism initiatives often involve local communities. Tour operators collaborate with communities to develop immersive experiences, such as guided village tours or homestays, allowing tourists to connect with locals and contribute to community development.

Promotion of Sustainable Activities: Portugal promotes eco-friendly and sustainable activities for tourists, such as hiking, birdwatching, and eco-tours. These activities encourage a deeper appreciation for nature and foster a sense of responsibility towards the environment.

Education and Awareness: The country invests in educating tourists about responsible behavior. Brochures, websites, and informational campaigns inform visitors about local customs, environmental regulations, and the importance of sustainable tourism.

Partnerships and Collaborations: Portugal collaborates with international organizations, NGOs, and other countries to exchange best practices and knowledge in responsible tourism.

This helps the country stay updated on the latest trends and strategies in sustainable tourism.

Regulation and Enforcement: Portugal enforces regulations related to responsible tourism through inspections and penalties for non-compliance. This ensures that businesses adhere to sustainable practices and contribute positively to the local environment and communities.

Investment in Renewable Energy: The country's focus on renewable energy, such as wind and solar power, not only reduces its carbon footprint but also demonstrates its commitment to sustainable practices.

These comprehensive responsible tourism initiatives in Portugal reflect the nation's dedication to preserving its natural beauty, cultural heritage, and quality of life for both residents and visitors alike.

Eco-friendly Accommodation

Eco-friendly accommodation in Portugal refers to lodging options that prioritize environmental sustainability and minimize their ecological footprint. Portugal, known for its stunning landscapes and rich cultural heritage, has embraced the concept of ecotourism and sustainable travel. Here are some comprehensive details about eco-friendly accommodation options in Portugal:

Certifications and Practices: Many eco-friendly accommodations in Portugal adhere to recognized sustainability certifications like EarthCheck, Green Key, and Biosphere Responsible Tourism. These certifications ensure that the accommodation follows specific environmental, social, and economic criteria, such as energy and water conservation, waste reduction, and support for local communities.

Types of Eco-Friendly Accommodation: Portugal offers a range of eco-friendly lodging options, including:

- **Eco-Lodges**: These are purpose-built accommodations designed with sustainable materials, energy-efficient designs, and minimal impact on the environment.
- **Agro-Tourism and Rural Tourism:** Staying at working farms or traditional rural homes allows travelers to experience local life while supporting local agriculture.
- **Glamping**: Glamorous camping combines luxury and nature, offering unique experiences without harming the environment.
- **Sustainable Hotels and Resorts**: Some hotels have adopted eco-friendly practices,

such as using renewable energy, recycling, and reducing water consumption.
- **Energy and Water Efficiency:** Eco-friendly accommodations in Portugal often use renewable energy sources like solar panels, wind turbines, or hydroelectric power. They also implement water-saving measures such as low-flow faucets, rainwater harvesting, and wastewater treatment systems.
- **Waste Reduction and Recycling**: These accommodations typically prioritize waste reduction by minimizing single-use plastics and promoting recycling programs. Some might even have on-site composting facilities.
- **Local Sourcing and Cuisine:** Eco-friendly accommodations often emphasize local sourcing of food and products, supporting nearby communities and reducing carbon emissions associated with transportation.
- **Wildlife Conservation and Biodiversity**: Many eco-lodges and accommodations are located in areas rich in biodiversity. They may participate in conservation programs and offer guided nature tours to educate guests about local flora and fauna.
- **Community Involvement**: Sustainable accommodations in Portugal often engage with local communities, providing

employment opportunities and supporting cultural preservation.
- **Educational and Recreational Activities:** Eco-friendly accommodations may organize eco-tours, workshops, and outdoor activities that promote sustainable practices and help guests connect with the natural surroundings.
- **Transportation**: These accommodations may encourage the use of eco-friendly transportation options, such as biking, walking, or using public transportation.
- **Design and Architecture**: Some eco-lodges are designed with minimal environmental impact in mind, utilizing bioclimatic architecture and integrating seamlessly into the natural landscape.

When planning a trip to Portugal, consider staying at one of these eco-friendly accommodations to not only enjoy a unique and immersive experience but also contribute to the preservation of Portugal's natural beauty and cultural heritage.

Chapter 7: Essential Portuguese Phrases

Basic Expressions

Basic Expressions in Portugal refers to common phrases and greetings used in the Portuguese language. Here are a few basic expressions along with their English translations:
Olá! (Hello!)
Bom dia! (Good morning!)
Boa tarde! (Good afternoon!)
Boa noite! (Good evening/night!)
Como está? (How are you?)
Estou bem, obrigado/a. (I'm fine, thank you.)
Por favor. (Please.)
Obrigado/a. (Thank you.)
De nada. (You're welcome.)
Desculpe. (Excuse me/I'm sorry.)
Sim. (Yes.)
Não. (No.)
Com licença. (Excuse me.)
Quanto custa? (How much does it cost?)
Pode falar mais devagar? (Can you speak more slowly?)
Não compreendo. (I don't understand.)
Onde fica...? (Where is...?)
À esquerda. (On the left.)
À direita. (On the right.)

Uma cerveja, por favor. (A beer, please.)

These basic expressions will help you navigate simple interactions and conversations in Portugal. Remember that pronunciation is key when speaking Portuguese, so try to practice and mimic the sounds as accurately as possible.

Shopping and Souvenirs

Portugal, a country rich in history, culture, and natural beauty, offers a diverse and captivating shopping experience for both locals and tourists. From bustling markets and charming boutiques to modern shopping centers, Portugal has something to offer every type of shopper. Additionally, the country's unique souvenirs reflect its distinctive heritage, making them cherished keepsakes for visitors.

Shopping Experience:
- **Traditional Markets**: Portugal is famous for its vibrant and bustling markets, where you can immerse yourself in the local culture and find a wide range of goods. The Mercado da Ribeira in Lisbon and the Mercado do Bolhão in Porto are two iconic markets that offer fresh produce, regional delicacies, handicrafts, and more.
- **Shopping Streets:** Portuguese cities are dotted with charming shopping streets lined

with boutiques, galleries, and local shops. In Lisbon, the **Avenida da Liberdade** is renowned for its luxury brands, while the historic district of **Baixa** offers a mix of traditional and contemporary stores.
- **Shopping Centers**: For those who prefer a modern shopping experience, Portugal boasts numerous shopping centers such as Amoreiras Shopping Center in Lisbon and NorteShopping in Porto. These centers house a variety of international and local brands, along with entertainment options like cinemas and restaurants.
- **Craftsmanship and Artisanal Goods:** Portugal has a long tradition of craftsmanship, producing high-quality items such as azulejos (ceramic tiles), intricate ceramics, handwoven textiles, and delicate lace. You can find these authentic products in specialty shops and markets across the country.

Souvenirs:
- **Azulejos**: These vibrant ceramic tiles are a hallmark of Portuguese artistry. They come in various designs and sizes, depicting scenes from history, nature, and daily life. Azulejos make for stunning decorative pieces or unique wall art to take home.

- **Port Wine**: A trip to Portugal wouldn't be complete without indulging in its world-famous Port wine. You can purchase bottles of this sweet, fortified wine from cellars in Porto or specialized wine shops.
- **Cork Products**: Portugal is the world's largest producer of cork, and you'll find an array of cork-based products, including bags, wallets, hats, and even clothing. These eco-friendly items are not only stylish but also a sustainable choice.
- **Filigree Jewelry**: Portuguese filigree is a delicate and intricate style of jewelry-making. Pieces often feature twisted and soldered threads of gold or silver, resulting in elegant and timeless ornaments.
- **Traditional Ceramics:** Hand-painted ceramics, such as plates, bowls, and tiles, showcase Portugal's artistic heritage. The city of Coimbra is particularly famous for its vibrant blue and white ceramics.
- **Sardine Tins**: Playful and decorative tins of canned sardines have become a popular souvenir in Portugal. These tins feature creative designs and make for amusing keepsakes.
- **Fado Music**: Fado, Portugal's soulful music genre, has a deep cultural significance. You can bring home Fado music albums or related merchandise to remember the emotional melodies and expressive lyrics.

- **Traditional Embroidery**: Portuguese embroidery, often featuring intricate designs and vibrant colors, is used to create beautiful textiles, linens, and clothing.

Shopping and souvenirs in Portugal offer a wonderful way to connect with the country's rich history, culture, and craftsmanship. Whether you explore the traditional markets, stroll along shopping streets, or discover hidden boutiques, you'll find a wide array of unique items to bring back home as cherished memories of your time in this enchanting country.

Printed in Great Britain
by Amazon